CREDO

CREDO

STEWART EDWARD WHITE

www.whitecrowbooks.com

Credo.

First published in 1925 by Doubleday, Page and Co.
This copyright © 2025 by White Crow Productions Ltd. All rights reserved.
Published by White Crow Books, an imprint of White Crow Productions Ltd.

A CIP catalogue record for this book is available from the British Library.
For information, contact White Crow Books by e-mail: info@whitecrowbooks.com.

Cover Design by Astrid@Astridpaints.com
Interior design by Velin@Perseus-Design.com

Paperback: ISBN: 9781786772701
eBook: ISBN: 9781786772718

Non-Fiction / BODY, MIND & SPIRIT / Afterlife & Reincarnation

www.whitecrowbooks.com

ACKNOWLEDGMENT

~

Naturally this book represents fairly wide reading in a great many fields of thought. It is impossible to nominate the ancestry, more or less remote, of any one or any set of ideas, though that ancestry may recall itself or hint at itself to a reader here and there.

Certain definite and outstanding conceptions owe their beginnings to especial sources, however. The beautifully compact expression of the quality of consciousness was first formulated in *Our Unseen Guest*. Frameworks of argument for specific details I have sometimes borrowed—as Geley on instincts; and Professor Clifford Farr on the distinctions between living and non-living creatures. To them and to the unnamed—and in some cases forgotten—who have supplied mental aliment, I make my bow.

One hundred years after this book was first published, I have taken the liberty of adding a Table of Contents for ease of navigation (Ed.).

CONTENTS

PREFACE

⌒

This book is intended to fulfil three divergent functions. It is an attempt to aid in the orientation among the bewildering new conditions of the century: it is an attempt to admit fresh ventilation to modern thought: it is a stretching exercise. Its result I hope will be to help the average man define his own beliefs.

CHAPTER 1

FINDING A BELIEF

~

1

AT some period in his life every thinking man must establish his own basic relations with the universe, or remain restless, discontented, and unhappy. He must get himself a genuine *belief*. A great many people do not do this, to be sure; but it must be acknowledged that a great many people go into an increasingly discontented old age.

Not long ago, at a dinner party, a woman and a typical square-jawed, literal-minded, bulldog businessman happened to touch upon religion. The man was stating impatiently that he could not find in theology or the literal doctrines of the church much that he could accept.

"Do you find you can get on satisfactorily without religion" asked the woman.

"That's just it!' he cried, surprisingly, "I can't!"

This man had come to a realization of the necessity for search; but—as yet—had got no further. There are at the present day thousands upon thousands like him.

What is this pressing necessity, in fundamental? It is the necessity in some way, satisfactory to each particular person, to account for things. Man must explain the universe, as far as he is able. He must define it. He must try to make rational its make-up, and its laws, and the trend of its movement. He must determine his own place in that universe, and his relation to it. And, above all, if he cannot account to himself for its origin and its purpose, he must at least be satisfied that its remote inceptions are an orderly projection in the past, and that it has a purpose. To make the job of living worthwhile, in deeper satisfaction, he must ask himself what it means, and he must have made a serious effort to answer.

His efforts at the answer are recorded in the mass of known science, and in a great multitude of beliefs. All are equally parts of the great attempt to place himself, and to find out what it is all about.

Now I am going to make a statement that may at first seem paradoxical. All faiths that have been sincerely worked out in the travail of a spirit groping toward this necessity, and have been sincerely believed, have been at some time true, no matter how false later progress may have shown them to be. That is not quite as foolish as it sounds. Every formulation that has held mankind's full credence has been based upon, or contained to the extent of its capacity, certain simple fundamental truths which are invariably the same. I shall not attempt to name them here.

The change of creeds, the abandonment of old beliefs and the adoption of new, have been rather the extension, the expansion, the enrichment of these fundamental truths. The new creed sees in no respect a different truth, but simply more of the old truth. We are finding, not a new magnetic north, but a fresh orientation necessitated by the fact that we have shifted our position. If we have not changed our position, we need no orientation.

We are happy in mind, and we do our jobs effectively—whatever they may be—only when we have figured out what it is all about *to the extent necessary to satisfy us.* We may, if we are a primitive people, be satisfied to account for things between markers set very close together, and we may be perfectly content to take on trust—"on faith"—whatever lies outside of these markers. But it may be said with confidence that between them must lie all the facts of our exact knowledge. If some of these facts stand outside the markers, unrelated, unaccounted for, we are never really at ease with ourselves. That is why our *credos* change and grow, because we are constantly learning more and more. With our increased body of knowledge the old faiths become inadequate. That by no means implies that the old faiths are "untrue," in the sense that it is untrue that fire is cold. It only means that as avenues of approach toward the portion of fundamental truth we are capable of containing

4

they are no longer open. A road is a road as long as it leads somewhere and is passable. It ceases to be a road otherwise. Fire may be cold in relation to the incandescence of a star. Details of creed become ridiculous to us only because we no longer see through them to the living thing, because they no longer in any way represent to us what in essence they have represented to others. We merely have different mechanisms, so to speak, to make us aware of exactly the same thing these "ridiculous" beliefs revealed to those others.

There we touch the difference between absolute and relative, which is, I admit, an extremely abstruse consideration, and almost impossible for the human and individualistic mind to grasp practically. We are inclined to reason that a specific thing either is so, or is not so; and if our superior knowledge of fact tells us that it is manifestly impossible that human life, for example, is conditioned by the arbitrary intervention of a theocracy of personal gods and goddesses living on Mt. Olympus, we state categorically that those who so believed were dwelling in complete error. I purposely take an example from the noncontroversial past, though the same reasoning could be quite well applied to the present day.

We could with greater justice admit that in his personal gods the Greek was seeing clearly just so much of certain cosmic influences as the needs of his state of development required. We need and see and use a greater portion of those influences, perhaps, and see them in different form; but they are identically the same influences in kind, and they orient us in the same direction.

"Oh, yes," you will often hear someone say, "There was a Jot of truth in most of those old beliefs. What people don't understand is that a great deal of it was allegorical."

That is not it at all. A great deal of them have *become* allegorical. But at the time they were true, literally true, as respects what then shone through them and for which they stood as representation.

2

The present time has produced a new need for Orientation. Our position has shifted enormously.

We have been learning so rapidly that almost more things stand outside the old limit markers than are included within. Evolution is one of the big things; and the processes by which it is carried on,—especially the proof of mutation. Evidently, in view of the latter, the old Darwinian theory of satisfactorily unbroken succession will not do. The Missing Link is missing because he never was. The spark leaped a gap. How could that happen? The electron is another of the big things, by which apparently matter is to be reduced to a single thing, and that thing a force. Chemical-psychology—or psychological-chemistry, whichever you please—has opened a whole world of parallelism, behaviorism, mechanistic response, which many people seem to fear is final. Psychical research is slowly de-occultizing the "sacred" to the combative dismay of many who seem to think a "miracle" is any less a miracle because it can be understood. The microscope, the telescope, the spectroscope, in the swift development of their modifications and improvements in delicacy, have revealed a huge catalogue of unexpected and somewhat disconcerting facts. Things are not quite as we supposed them. They will not take their places inside the old limit markers.

Now all these things are tremendously fascinating. As soon as they are translatable to common speech, they—or some specialty from among them—are eagerly seized upon by the man in the street. Truth is not only stranger than fiction; it is more interesting than fiction. Given a specialist who has sufficiently surrounded and digested some aspect of his subject so that he can tell it in common speech, he is sure of an audience. Digested and understood science does not need to be abstruse, except one desires to follow processes of arrival as well as results. Dr. Milliken on the electron, Sir Oliver Lodge on the ether of space, Fabre or Maeterlinck on the polity of the insect world, Sir Arthur Keith on the mechanism of the human body, to mention but a few, are as clear as crystal and interesting to even the seasoned novel reader, if one can induce that person to make a start. Thomson's *Outline of Science* has already gone through innumerable editions.

But also these things are terribly disconcerting to the old beliefs. They cannot fail to be for they present a great variety of things unaccounted for in the specific terms of the old faiths.

To be sure there are a great many to whom this orientation presents no difficulty. They are able to recognize that their old creed does actually comprehend these new things in what seems to others an allegorical sense; but which to them is still a real sense. They have moved closer to the old laws, as one might say, in order to cover a wider field. They are satisfied that the cosmos—including these new things—is still accounted for in the old formulations. Therefore they are happy in the terms of their religion, to which they are still able to accord that full and heartfelt belief that is necessary to happiness.

But the most of us have not that beautiful power of interpretation. We require things to be more specifically stated. Meaning, perhaps, comes to us more through the words of ordered thought than through the subtler channels of spiritual perception. A new formulation, a new orientation is imperatively necessary; and until it is gained that necessity urges us.

3

It is a real necessity, and a driving necessity. Until we have accounted for things we cannot go on, either individually or collectively; not with any satisfaction to ourselves nor benefit to the scheme of things. I presume in due course we will make what might be called a new formulation that will resemble a creed—something which the majority of us will be satisfied fits all the basic facts we have attained to at this time; something elastic enough also to adjust to individual points of view. It will be true, just as the gods of Olympus were true. In the meantime each individual must do his best to work it out for himself.

This is an attempt to set forth how one man has worked it out for himself. It is offered as what seems to him a rational accounting for things inside the limit markers of his present knowledge. Perhaps it may appeal to others and so help them to settle in an orientation spot from which they also can satisfactorily contemplate life, and by which they can ascribe to it a reasonable meaning. Perhaps it may suggest to others, elements which will help them in their own construction. It is my formulation, satisfactory to myself, at the present time, of the fundamentals expressed in terms of present day knowledge.

Now any belief, no matter how crude, always has to do with the nature of things. So must this.

And as we have by no means reached the limit of our exact knowledge of things themselves, any belief must go beyond exact knowledge. It will always be that way. We must have the courage to extend our straight lines into outer space. It is not always sufficient to stick to the weighed and measured facts. We must postulate probabilities; as science has postulated the ether which all attempted experiment has as yet failed to *prove*, as the atom has been proved. Yet the atom was a pure postulation of the Greeks. The only real proof of any belief must be what might be called the cosmic satisfaction it conveys. Its only possible criterion can be as to whether or not it fits the case, fully and completely and convincingly.

CREDO

The following view of the nature of things has come to satisfy me, at least as a temporary belief. Perhaps there will be some who have reached the same position as myself. Or perhaps—what is more likely—something here expressed may help others to reach their own position.

CHAPTER 2

THE BEGINNING OF CONSCIOUS INQUIRY

~

1

THE first question that man asks of himself has to do with the nature of the things about him. The one fact he is sure of is that of his own existence. He can state with conviction *I am*. That is the bedrock bottom of his certainty, and is common to all philosophies.

But soon he discovers in one way or another that this is not sufficient. His self-awareness depends on the existence of other things from which to be different. He cannot conceive of himself as deprived of all external correspondence whatever. His curiosity as well as his self-interest demands that he first of all account for these things, by which he is surrounded, and to which he reacts. What are they? What relation do they bear to each other? Whence came they? What place among men does he himself occupy?

These questions he must answer according to his capacity and within the limit markers he sets for himself intelligently, or which are set for him by his limitations. Most limits are of the latter class, and he is unaware of their existence until they have been overpassed and he can look back at them. But some he deliberately sets for himself. A familiar and early example of that is exhibited by the child looking upward to the sky. He cannot conceive of there being no end to the space directly above his head; and yet at the same time, if he limits it with a wall, he cannot conceive of there being no space beyond the wall. There can be no end, and yet the nature of his mind demands an end. Never does he puzzle long over that matter before deliberately he plants one of his markers. It is an insoluble riddle. He gives it up, and turns his attention nearer home.

He looks about him more closely, and sees that the world does not appear to be functioning very well. There is pain, and injustice, and cruelty, and war, and fruitless labor, and poverty, and the iron necessities of heredity. Things seem to be in a mess. And yet some instinct within him continues to hope, and some force within him continues to struggle. Are that instinct and that force real things? Are they justifiable? If so, how? What is it all about?

All serious philosophic or religious systems occupy themselves with an attempt to answer these questions. They vary much in character and direction, they succeed because of the truth they contain, and they wane and finally disappear because they have viewed the truth from too narrow an angle. They have too much occupied themselves with one aspect, ignoring many others that must be taken into consideration for even an approximate balance. Religion of the middle ages thus ignored or denied the facts of science.

Science until very recently has not taken into consideration the imponderables: it is beginning to do so only reluctantly, partially, and in special directions. Mysticism has not satisfied. Man thinks he rejects pure mysticism because it is not clearly connected with the solid life that is his job. In reality he rejects it, as he finally has rejected other answers, because it is speaking only in terms of itself, because it fails to take into consideration—to account for—all the others.

Nevertheless, mysticism is an essential part of the answer. I mean true mysticism in its precise definition; I do not mean vagueness or "fuzziness," which is what the word connotes to most. Without it as a component part in proper proportion we have only a mechanism which does not explain even itself. The greater scientists themselves have never attempted to dispose of mysticism. They have not argued for a final mechanism. A careful reading of Huxley, Tyndall, Spencer—the leading originators of the scientific attitude—will show that in the last analysis they advocated the rigid use of materialistic accuracy and concentration on materialistic research in order at last to translate the essential mysticism into the terms of the known. The symbols of the known are the symbols of science. When all is said and done, when all the measurements and weighings, and determinations of exact science—whether in chemistry, physics, psychology and their kin—are for the moment finished; when, again for the moment, we know all we can know about the physical constitution of that by which we are surrounded and of which we are a part, then we must tackle once more the real problem, that of expressing the essential mysticism in the terms of science, in the terms of the known. That is the only language we can speak which will ultimately satisfy us.

2

Stripped to the bone we try to know things along three lines—what is the material of which we and the things about us are made? What is the life that animates them? What is the consciousness by which we become aware of them and of ourselves? We have no ultimate knowledge of any of these things, but we have pushed back considerably our limit markers of relative knowledge.

Are we justified in considering the lines of our knowledge as straight lines which can with confidence be theoretically extended? Do they tend to converge?

Whatever the answer, this does seem to me indisputable; that the truth cannot be expressed wholly in terms of any one of the three. Not with the sort of satisfaction I have called cosmic, the sort that carries with it a sense of the deeper as distinguished from the intellectual conviction. The mechanistically inclined scientist may be inescapably pushed by the logic of what he sees and knows to a conviction of a wholly material and mechanistic universe; but he accepts his conclusion sadly and with reluctance. The theological doctrinaire whose literalness does violence to his common sense leads a divided existence wherein his workaday life is paralleled by an ideal but "impractical" religion. He believes the Sermon on the Mount with one half of himself, and does business with the other. To be satisfying the Answer must comprehend frankly and fully all that we know.

3

In order even to state the problem to ourselves, then, we are forced to review, however briefly, what we do know. And at once we are astounded at the extent to which science has of late done its share toward producing what we might call handleable simplicities.

Not long ago we had our seventy-two "irresolvable" elements of which the physical universe was composed. These were separate and distinct and unlike things, whose combination made all other substances. They themselves must have been "created" as individual things. We had gained, to be sure, an insight into their structure. They were made up of molecules which were in turn composed of atoms. But these molecules and atoms were themselves the same substance as the element. We had hydrogen atoms, and uranium atoms and tellurium atoms, and so on. They represented rather the limits of minuteness into which a given substance could be divided, rather than the material of which that substance was made.

But within a fairly recent date the discovery of the electron has upset this earlier conception. Let us attempt to strip the subject of its technical aspects, and see if we cannot make a simple picture that will not be too inaccurate.

The atom, it seems, is composed of constituents even smaller than itself; and these constituents *are all the same thing* even for the atoms of diverse elements. Furthermore these constituents seem to be—at least predominantly—forces rather than substances. They are positive and negative charges of electricity. We have called these charges of electricity out of which the atoms of definite substances are made, electrons and protons, or nuclei. The electron is the negative charge, and the proton is the positive charge.

How then do these electrons and protons, which are in turn only one thing, manage to combine to produce the eighty-eight known elements, from whose combinations in turn are made up the thousands of substances in our cosmos?

It is a question of number, and perhaps of speed. Around a nucleus consisting of a positive charge revolve in orbits, like infinitesimal solar systems, a greater or smaller number of electrons. This number, and arrangement, and—as we have said,—perhaps the speed of revolution, determine the atom.[1] Thus hydrogen, the simplest of all elements, is composed of a proton around which, in a circular orbit, revolves one electron. The most complicated atom, that of uranium, is a system in which ninety-two electrons revolve in intricate orbits about the central nucleus. Between the two there is practically an unbroken progression.

---

[1] The number of revolving electrons, strictly speaking, indicates the amount of the positive changes in the nucleus, and under certain conditions may vary or be absent—as when the nucleus is positively electrified. However, in normal condition the above statement is correct, and will be retained for the sake of clarity.

The hydrogen atom, as we have seen, is composed of a single electron revolving about its nucleus, proton: helium of two; lithium of three; glucinum of four; and so on. A few gaps exist. We do not know of any atom composed of forty-three electrons revolving about the nucleus; nor of seventy-five; nor of eighty-four, eighty-five, eighty-seven, and eighty-nine. But as the progression is otherwise unbroken, it is reasonable to suppose that we shall somewhere in the physical universe discover elements to correspond. Indeed we have already filled in some of the gaps that existed when the list was first made out. Chromium is a case in point. No element made up of atoms whose composition is of twenty-four electrons in revolution was known until it was first determined as existing in the surface of the sun.

However that may be, it is important to observe that atoms of the most diverse substances differ from each other only in the number—and possibly the speed—of free electrons revolving in the orbit of their miniature solar systems. If by some means copper were to lose one of its electrons it would become nickel; or if it were to gain one from some outside source it would become zinc. A true transmutation would have taken place.

So much has been thoroughly proved. We average men find difficulty at first in comprehending how a thing like the electron can possibly be weighed and counted and measured. If we could expand everything in our world except ourselves to ten billion times its present size, an atom would be about three feet in diameter, but the electrons in it would be only about as big as a pin head! That such a thing can actually be handled by scientific instruments almost strains our credulity.

Nevertheless, it has not only been done in a variety of ways, but the results have been repeated in various laboratories all over the world. Though the processes are in themselves fascinating, we cannot go into them here. The reader, if interested, must go to original sources.[2]

Beyond the proven facts are certain speculations so reasonable that we may with considerable confidence adopt them as working hypotheses, and may look forward to their ultimate proof. This transmutation by the addition to or the subtraction from the number of free electrons in an atom of matter is constantly taking place. It has also been noted that the more complex the structure of the atom, the heavier it is. There appears to be a gradual building up, a sort of inorganic evolution. Each

---

[2] Suggested: Milliken—The Electron. Lodge—The Electron. Russell—The ABC of Atoms.

element may have sprung from the element next simpler. Antimony with fifty-one electrons may by the addition of one more have given birth to tellurium with fifty-two; and antimony may therefore well have *preceded* tellurium in the history of the universe. Thus we may logically conceive of the physical cosmos as at first consisting of hydrogen only; then of hydrogen and helium; then of hydrogen, helium and lithium, and so on. Since this progressively complex type of evolution has been found to obtain botanically, zoologically, psychologically,—indeed in about all fields of investigation—it is more than probable that it also obtains in pure physics. This view receives also considerable experimental corroboration.

But in the dazzlement of this brilliant new light of knowledge we must not be blinded to the fact that we have rather a simplification than anything resembling an ultimate explanation. It is very difficult to conceive of "atoms of electricity as a pure disembodied force," without *some* vehicle of manifestation, however attenuated. Many physicists try to explain protons and electrons as vortices in the ether of space. As it is obvious that a vortex can be either right or left handed, there is room in this hypothesis for the two sorts of electricity—positive and negative: the proton and the electron. In that case we still have our duality. It is pushed very far back, but it still exists: the ether that revolves, and the energy that revolves it. And we still must inquire as to what sets that revolution in motion. The vehicle of manifestation has attenuated almost to the vanishing point, where before it has held an equal importance; the force has become important almost to the usurpation of the whole field. The primal cause is as mysterious as ever.

4

There is an interesting corollary which we should not pass by. We have said that there seems to be an organic evolution by which an increasing complexity of substance is produced in orderly sequence by the addition of electrons to already existing simpler atoms. There is also indubitably an accompanying simplification, a breaking down of the complex atom. Indeed it is the latter process, rather than the former, of which we are most cognizant in process. We can observe and evaluate the release of energy this activity brings about; we are gauging its effects in all directions; and we are coming more and more to a utilization of what we have loosely designated as one form of radio activity. For that is what the simplification of substance amounts to.

Probably every bit of matter in the universe—irrespective of its kind—displays to a greater or lesser degree some radio activity. That is to say constantly from the incredible trillions of electrons that compose its mass a certain relatively small number are continually disengaging themselves and flying forth. The release of energy thus brought about; the collisions, the re-amalgamations, the various hazards and ultimate fate of these adventurers is not our concern just now. But were this process unhindered or unmodified, there must come a point when enough of them will have been withdrawn sufficiently to have altered the proportion between the number of electrons and the central nucleus in the atoms of that particular substance so that the substance itself will change to a simpler substance. This must in the nature of things be brought about very gradually, so gradually that we cannot say that it takes place under our eyes. An analogy might be realized by imagining two ten thousand gallon tanks of water balanced at either end of a gigantic beam. One of the tanks leaks, a drop at a time. Naturally not one drop, nor two, nor ten thousand will affect the equilibrium of the tanks; but if the leak continues long enough it is inevitable that sooner or later the beam will incline. In a similar manner, although it is probable that every substance of which the universe is composed is radioactive—is constantly sending forth its stream of free electrons—nevertheless, the amount sent forth is so small proportionately to the whole that the equilibrium of the substance is not immediately destroyed. There is a tendency, however, and perhaps a process of a breaking down from the complex heavier atom to the simpler lighter atom. Mercury tends by this means to become gold; gold, platinum; platinum, iridium; and so on down the list.

Thus we see two processes constantly going on, a building up from the simpler structures to the complex; and a breaking down or dissolving the complex into the simple. Both are processes natural to, inherent in, the composition of matter itself.

5

It seems to be evident that at this period in time the first process has the preponderance. We have charted our evolution sufficiently to understand that anything we examine, whether solar systems or animal life, whether chemical constituent or mind, has invariably started its career in simplicity and worked up through constant accretion and specialization to a present complexity. Furthermore that process is continuing to a further complexity. That is what we have understood by evolution. Whatever coincidental breaking down of atoms—or anything else—there may have been or may be, the building up is so far in excess that the net result is more things and more complicated things rather than less things and simpler things.

Physical manifestations—or, indeed, mental or psychical manifestations—are more numerous as time goes on.

Nevertheless as a natural property of matter as we know it, and not at all as what we call degeneration, the possibility of simplification exists. Just as the eighty odd physical elements seem, from one point of view, to have been built up step by step from a simple opposition of one electron and a positively charged nucleus to ninety-two electrons and a nucleus; so it is entirely possible, by the orderly and continuous dispersion of electrons in radio activity, for those presumably ninety-two elements successively to disappear. Beginning with uranium, the altering of balance might very well proceed down through UX3, thorium, the unknown "89," radium and the rest, until once more we theoretically contemplate hydrogen with its simple "one and one" structure as the last remaining element of all. As our evolution has proceeded from the extremely simple to the complex; so, *by the same law,* it may be said to be capable of evolving from the complex to the simple.

No philosophical view that does not take this into count may be considered even approximately complete. And once we begin to take it into account we inevitably come upon a swarm of analogies. Indeed so numerous and universal are the analogies that we are almost forced to acknowledge the justness of their application. It is in essence the rounding of the circle. A man leaves home, and travels and adventures for many years, and returns at last to the exact point from which he started. He reads in youth one of the fundamental books—such as the Bible—and goes forth into the experience of life where he acquires wisdom; and reads again but with a new illumination the very same printed pages. He starts with the bare outlines of hypothesis, he loses himself in a maze of detailed experiment, he emerges at last with a clear scientific statement of fifty words. He accepts blindly a faith, and abandons its literalness, and makes his many studies and his first-hand observations, and returns with understanding to his faith again. Always this is to be noted; that though he returns it is always with a gain and an interpretation. The point to which he returns is the same from which he departed; but it is enriched and illuminated by his swing around the circle. The original simplicity is regained; but it is a simplicity *plus* the complex.

There seems scant need of elaborating this, for it is within the personal knowledge of every human being who has at all developed. Indeed, so universal is the experience that we are fairly justified in saying that any experience or subject of knowledge or faith that cannot be stated clearly in simple terms has not rounded out its circle, has not emerged from the complexity of its apogee to the simplicity of its perigee. A man still lost in the complicated is still on his journey, as far as that particular phase or subject is concerned.

But the immediate point of consideration is this: that if, as seems probable, the substantial universe as we see it, is going to be subject in time—by the action of the laws we have outlined—to a resimplification in material, so that gradually it will dissolve and disappear, that process will not be a death nor degeneration in the sense of a loss. It will be merely a closing of the circle, the regaining of simplicity with a function fulfilled. In the cycle of a great plan beyond the limit markers of our understanding it will be a return home with understanding.

CHAPTER 3

LIVE THINGS AND DEAD THINGS

~

1

B EFORE going on to examine further what we know about the matter from the physicist's standpoint, let us approach it from the other two angles—that of life, and of consciousness.

But we do not wish, as yet, to go very far into our examination of them; that will come later. For the moment it is sufficient to advance the concept that *all things are alive*, and that *all things have consciousness*, of some degree or another.

To some that concept will seem almost self-evident; to most it will appear to be ridiculous. It is entirely a question of the point of view, and largely of definition.

We have become accustomed to speak of "live things" and "dead things," and we know pretty well what we mean when we use these terms. But they are terms of convenience, merely, and not of exact definition. Indeed, they will not bear the simplest analysis.

Pressed to define living things the child or the primitive will reply vaguely that live things can move about. But there are plants. The definition and its refutation seem to us equally simple. Yet a more sophisticated attempt to draw the line between the living and the lifeless fares no better. There always interpose intermediary forms which will not fall under the terms of the definition, and which refuse to admit of a sharp division.

Let us examine things from the point of view of mere structure. Are living things and lifeless things differently made? Yes, say some, living things have a cellular structure: lifeless things have not.[1] This sounds interesting and possible. First of all, what is a cell? Classically a cell is a 'body of more or less uniform, definite shape and size, consisting of an enveloping layer (the plasma membrane) and an internal liquid (the cytoplasm), within which are two kinds of especial organs (the nucleus and vacuoles). But at once we are called to consider the blue-green alge, a true plant, but without nuclei. Then there are the plasmodia of slime molds. These also have no nuclei, and hence are not composed of cells in the classic sense.

Suppose, then, as Farr suggests, we redefine the word cell, omitting the nucleus, and the item of approximate uniformity. Then we could, for this purpose, say that a cell is a body consisting of a plasma membrane (the envelope), and cytoplasm (the internal liquid). But recent microscopic studies have shown us that even this will not do. There are junctures in the life-histories of certain bacteria—the malarial is one—when it is pure plasmodium; and some fungi, among plants, are supposed by many botanists to pass through a similar state. And even more striking in this respect are what are called the filterable viruses. These viruses, as far as known, pass all their lives in a completely liquid condition, having no structural form whatever; and yet they behave in about the same way as do similar microscopic organisms of orthodox cellular construction.

So if we are to segregate living from lifeless in terms of cellular structure merely, we are forced to redefine the cell as a liquid! In other words, the distinction, so far as structure is concerned, disappears.

But these same filterable viruses open another door. No one has been able to determine any difference whatever in structure between them and the enzymes, and very little if any difference in their behavior. Enzymes accomplish the digestive operations and other chemical changes in the body. They originate in living beings, but they may exist and operate outside of living beings. They are supposed to be colloids, and colloids have no necessary connection with life, either in origin, existence, or behavior. They are simply definite aggregates of molecules of either organic or inorganic substances. Molecules, of course, are composed of atoms.

Now with structure as the criterion where is one going to draw the line? We have cells, plasmodia, mycoplastic conditions, the filterable

---

[1] Farr: The Mind of the Molecule. Atlantic Monthly, Oct. 1923.

viruses, enzymes, colloids, molecules, atoms. Considered structurally, which is which, and which is not?

2

How about chemistry? Can that help us out? Can its laboratories give us an analysis that will definitely establish the difference between the living and the lifeless? We have found that there is no structural difference between the "living" and the lifeless: is there a chemical difference? It appears not. At one time the theory was held that all living things were composed of one chemical compound which was named protoplasm. Today it is known that protoplasm is, as far as chemistry is concerned, simply salts and water and various organic compounds, none of which, either alone or in combination, are peculiar to living things. In other words, every single chemical element that occurs in living things occurs also in lifeless things. There is no substance, or combination of substances, of which we can say this is chemically stuff of which only "living" things are made.

3

But there are other criteria which must be considered. We might say that a "living" thing is one that utilizes or produces food: that it is one that grows: that it is one that reproduces itself.

The releasing of energy by the digestion of food can be very quickly dismissed. It is an oxidization, just as the burning of coal or wood is an oxidization. Both result in a release of energy. There is no clear cut dividing line here, even in process; for there seem to be "no intermediate steps taking place in organism which seems to be impossible elsewhere."

The manufacture of food has not been until recently quite so self-evident. It has seemed that only by life could the raw material of nature be turned into sustenance for other life. The vegetable kingdom has always been the great intermediary in this respect. But now certain chemists—among whom Emil Fischer, Stoklasa and Ewart are most prominently named—have in the past twenty years imitated chemically this process. The intermediation of life to produce food has been definitely proved to be theoretically unnecessary, however practically important it may be.

Similarly chemistry has succeeded in imitating or duplicating all the processes of the body having to do with absorption, conduction, secretion. Those processes are not the exclusive property of "living" things—unless all things are living. Neither is there here a clear dividing line.

But how about growth? That looks like a good basis for definition. A living thing is capable of growth: a "lifeless" thing is not. Let us see.

Growth consists of three things—cell division; cell enlargement; cell differentiation. These things have all been artificially imitated in non-living structures. The stone of the field may not grow, but the type of matter of which it is composed is capable of growth. Furthermore, that very type of matter has been made to grow experimentally. In other words, the material of which the stone is made is *capable* of growth. One cannot avoid the logic that if growth is a criterion of life, then anything capable of growth must be living, whether it exercises that capability or not. Or else growth as a criterion must be discarded.

The cell division type of growth Lehman demonstrated with liquid crystals. These divide and subdivide exactly as do the cells of bacteria.

Leduc[2] also even produced artificially all the stages of nuclear division in colloids,—which, it will be remembered, are classed as "lifeless" substances.[3]

Cell enlargement is demonstrated in "non-living" matter through an artificial cell invented by Traube, and named after him. One way of making a Traube cell is by dropping a crystal of copper sulphate into a solution of potassium ferrocyanide—a purely chemical and mechanical procedure. The result is a cell with a membrane, a contained "sap," and a nucleus-like central crystal. This manufactured cell will enlarge and change shape in a most remarkable series of forms that simulate those of fungi, mosses, and even some of the lower animals. It follows conditions just as the "living" cell enlarges or changes form according to conditions.

Yet scientists continue to raise interesting pets. Cell differentiation is another way of indicating internal structural change. It is not yet authoritatively demonstrated that this can be done artificially. Yet in 1923 Dr. E. J. Allen reported on the basis of experiments by Church and others, the sequence by which it seems more than probable that from sea water under the influence of light certain living cells come into being, which divide and enlarge and develop swimming organs and

[2] The Mechanism of Life.

[3] See also Bade in The Scientific American, March 1922.

feeding habits.[4] So though this case is still in the experimental stage, cell differentiation also seems in a fair way to losing its distinctive quality as an attribute of "living" things. At the lowest it becomes a slender and isolated distinction on which to depend.

With these experiments the reproductive faculty falls into second importance as a distinguishing characteristic, for at its most primitive reproduction is neither more nor less than cell division; and cell division, as we have seen, has been artificially induced in "non-living" structures. Nor need we be led astray by recent experiments that appear to show the bisexuality in what have been considered asexual entities. In the one celled animal—such as the paramoecium—and in the one celled plant—such as the diatom—two cells fuse to start the division into many. It has long been thought that these two fusing cells were identical. Now it is known by Blakselee's experiments with certain of the molds that the two fusing cells are physiologically different. He calls them plus and minus, and shows that a plus cell never fuses with a plus, nor a minus with a minus. He might as well have called them male and female.

This sexual characteristic of reproduction might at first glance seem to promise a basis of distinction between the "living" and the "non-living." It is necessary to examine whether the "non-living" does or does not parallel the same process. There remains much work to be done in this field before the demonstration may be considered exact; but the logical outline seems to be fairly well drawn. In purely chemical compounds the plus and minus have long been recognized. There are positive and negative ions, and no two positives can combine, nor two negatives.

And we must not forget the ultimate constitution of matter in the electron and the proton,—the positive and the negative. If sex reproduction is to be considered a sole characteristic of "living" things, it would almost seem that the burden of proof is on that side.

4

So our analysis shows that no criterion we have as yet succeeded in formulating enables us to distinguish anything whatever as being "living" or "non-living." Every characteristic of the "living" thing is to be found or can be reproduced in the "non-living" thing, if not in degree, then in kind. The property of life is in all types of matter.

---

[4] See Appendix I.

Now, with all the foregoing clearly in mind, it would be well to go back to original definitions for a moment. In the ultimate, as the physicists have shown us, physical substance itself is reduced to a proton in equilibrium with a greater or lesser number of revolving electrons. That revolution is taking place because of energy, force. Withdraw the force, stop the revolution in the infinitesimal orbit—were such a thing possible—what would happen? Necessarily the substance would be obliterated. No substance, however inert, can exist at all unless it is throughout every molecule, every atom of its being, vibrant with energy, with force. And this force can be no other than the vital principle,—life. It is of course an almost incredible simplification, when so viewed, as compared with the complex life that animates the human being. But so is primordial matter an almost incredible simplification as compared with the intricate substances of which the human body is composed. There is no difference. A lifeless thing is impossible.

5

The same considerations will be found to apply as to consciousness. At first blush we think we can define pretty accurately some things that have consciousness and others that have not. A man is conscious, a dog, an ant, or a bird or a bee. That is self-evident. A rock is not conscious, nor garden soil, nor a piece of wood: almost anybody would agree on that. How about a tree or a cabbage?

Not many years ago there would have been no doubt on that point either. But now even the layman is not so certain. Some members of the vegetable kingdom seem to act as though they were conscious; that is, they not only conduct their daily life according to a complicated plan, but they modify and adapt themselves to circumstances in a most astonishing manner. They actually display ingenuity. People talk about and write about the intelligence of the flowers as they write about the Intelligence of the bee, and there is not a great deal of difference either in the sort of phenomena described nor in the apparently actuating motives. Both seem to feel and act from a common point which we call instinct in order to name and so get rid of it. A short time ago we should not have thought of ascribing anything so nearly rational as instinct to a plant. But in view of the resourcefulness, adaptability, and apparently original ingenuity in overcoming the unexpected which late observations have revealed to us, we cannot reasonably distinguish some of these activities *in kind* from the instinctive activities of the insects. And from that point of view it is difficult to deny to the flower at least a modicum of the same sort of instinctive consciousness we have already conceded to the bee. We shall have more to say of that later.

This, of course, gets us nowhere. It is adduced here only to call attention to the fact that even in the average mind the limit of acknowledged consciousness has been pushed back and back, and is even now uncertain.

But when one states that not only has a stone of the field or a bit of iron consciousness, but that it is the same sort of consciousness that you and I enjoy, then one's sense of humor rises. It is not a proposition that can be accepted on sight. When made acceptable, it must be shown to be literally and not merely figuratively true. In order to understand, we must first of all define consciousness.

Considered through its essence and not merely through its attributes, it may be defined quite simply as that power by which anything becomes aware of itself. We have dealt with that before. But in order to become aware of itself there must be an external thing from which it differs and to which it must be related. It is, in other words, by being aware of something different from oneself, that one knows that one is a separate being. Philosophically viewed that something different may conceivably be very close to the center of being—a mere subjective response to stimulus—but the stimulus must exist. The ultimate of certainty of which human thought is capable is the conviction that one is *I am*. But that conviction can only come by the reaction of *I am* to something beside itself.

That much is clear enough. But it must not be forgotten that to appreciate the existence of the something different some sort of apparatus is necessary. We must possess something to receive the stimulus. That also is self-evident. We will call this something, broadly, the "awareness-mechanism."

Now turn the proposition inside out. We have seen that it is through its reaction to something outside itself by means of an awareness-mechanism that the *I am* is conscious. Conversely, it follows that a response to anything outside itself, through a mechanism, must imply consciousness. The conclusion is inescapable. It may be a degree of consciousness that is very slight as compared to the consciousness we know in ourselves. The quality of it may differ from our own as widely as the quality of the hydrogen atom differs from the quality of our flesh structure. But it is the same kind of consciousness; just as the electrons and protons that make up the hydrogen atom are the same kind of electrons and protons that make up our body cells.

This much is clear enough, and would hardly be disputed. If we obtain through the physical mechanism of any entity a kick-back or reaction, I think we may fairly say that the entity may be said to be "aware" of the stimulus. The fact of its awareness is attested by the fact of its kick-back. That some of these reactions are extremely simple and are brought about by mechanical reflexes without—as far as we know—the intervention of intellectual intelligence does not really alter the case. The entity,—whatever it may be—holds within itself certain definite powers and also certain definite potentialities which make it what it is. When one of these characteristics—which, I must repeat, are individual—is touched, the response is made. And no stimulus which has not its receiving mechanism in the entity can have any effect whatever. In other words, the entity is aware of some things and not of others.[5]

Take any very simple and obvious specific example. The principle becomes plain at once.

The normal human being has five developed senses by which he responds to, is aware of, the physical world about him. But a man born blind can be aware through only four of them. As far as his reactions are concerned color and most properties of light do not exist at all. Nevertheless, light and color continue to surround him. In the fact that

---

[5] I find many of those who have been kind enough to read this confess to a confusion at this point. The simplest expression of this confusion may be thus stated: "Suppose I kick a stone. The stone will respond by rolling.

That, according to your argument, would indicate consciousness because of response. Yet the force applied was entirely my own, and the stone's apparent 'response' was illusory." The answer is, of course, that the stone's response in rolling was not primarily to the kick, but to the force of gravitation. The kick merely supplied a condition. The true response was to the state of equilibrium.

Another expression of the same difficulty was this: "Take the motor car. It moves and functions and reacts in response to law. Would you then say that the automobile is a conscious thing?" Certainly not, as an automobile. As a matter of fact, the machine is a cunningly assembled artificial aggregation of many sorts of responses,—of gasoline atoms to ignition, of mutual attractions of gravitation, of tensions, of response to the necessity for equilibrium, etc. One might say that a number of consciousnesses are harnessed together by man's intelligence to produce a correlated result. The trouble really is that the readers have not sufficiently distinguished between mere awareness— as evidenced by reaction—and intellectual awareness, which is an entirely different thing of infinitely higher development.

he has no awareness-mechanism to deal with them he is individually different from his fellows.

Now let us deprive him successively of hearing, of taste, of smell, leaving him only the sense of touch. Nevertheless—though in a very limited way—he is still cognizant of his own existence as a separate and individual being. He handles things; he experiences pain when burned; he is aware of movement. But now take away his power as to this last. Paralyze his limbs completely, yet leaving him the single and doubtful ability to receive sensory impressions. In none of these circumstances would we deny him what we call consciousness in even the narrow sense of the term. Through some awareness-mechanism, however diminished, he receives stimuli and responds to them, even though that response is entirely subjective, in a manner to show that he is self-aware.

Throughout all this process we have left him his intellectual power, and that has been an essential part of his awareness-mechanism. He has translated whatever diluted impressions he has been able to receive through an intellectual process, however abridged, into response, however feeble. Should we drug his brain into apathy, or by some other means sever it from supervision, we say that he has become unconscious, a being without consciousness. If then we touch his hand with a red-hot poker he, as an individual human entity, will fail to respond in any manner and will have ceased to be aware—simply because all physical awareness-mechanism lacks.[6] If we restore to him the power of movement, but leave him otherwise as before, his hand will twitch, or he will snatch it away. We call that a reflex action, but still define him as a being without consciousness, when he is considered as a complete human entity.

This course of reasoning must lead us provisionally to define consciousness as response to outside influence, through an awareness-mechanism, via some degree of intelligence.[7]

What, then, is intelligence? In the human being as also, of course, in at least the higher animals and the birds, it has to do with the brain.

---

[6] Of course as an aggregate of many smaller consciousnesses he still exists and is aware. Individual cells will respond, or individual aggregates of cells. His flesh can still be charred locally by fire; his finger will bleed. The restoration of the power of movement, indicated in the next sentence, merely shows a linking up of these separate aggregations by a certain small portion of the central being.

[7] Not necessarily intellectual intelligence!

It diminishes down through the animal kingdom to a very pinpoint of simplicity, but in careful analysis the distinction holds good until we get into the invertebrate and the microscopic. But how about the brain of the jellyfish? the brain of the rotifer? Does it exist, as we define it in the bird, or even the fish or the reptile? If it does not exist, are these creatures then unaware of themselves as separate individuals?

If we insist on the intellectual criterion we cannot say. But the intellectual criterion has, in fact, long since proved untenable. All down the line the center of significant reaction has been shifting from the brain to the spinal cord, from the spinal cord to the nerve centers. The transition has been gradual, the succession unbroken. We can fix no point at which we can definitely say, here intelligent action ceases and purely reflex instinctive action begins. One fades into the other so imperceptibly that we cannot draw a line. Our conception of intelligence must broaden. It comes at last to mean merely a response that is fitting, is in accordance with the scheme of things, that follows and corresponds to and fulfils an interplay in accordance with what we call natural law.

It is an inexorable logic from which we cannot escape. And when we retrace our steps, climbing once again up the long series that leads from the simple to the complex, from the rotifer back to man again, we perceive that as each response of any mechanism is necessarily in accordance with the law of its own being, so the brain itself must be merely *one kind* of awareness-mechanism which responds according to the law of its being also.

It produces one type of awareness by its reaction, according to its law, to what is outside itself. It gives a response—a very complicated response to be sure—to what can reach it; exactly as the tremendously simplified rotifer reacts in response to the few simple conditions that can affect it. The brain cannot react in any manner outside the laws of its structure and being, no more can the rotifer.

In this view it is not the kind of reaction that is important, it is the fact of reaction. The rotifer is sensitive of the existence of something outside itself; and it shows, within the limits of its equipment, that it is sensitive by the fact that it alters its action or condition in consonance. Its primitive little organism shows by its expansion .or shrinking or change of function that it has received the impression, that its mechanism is aware of the impression, and that an attempt is made to modify to meet the new conditions. The brain in a similar manner shows that it is aware by the fact that it alters its functioning in consonance with the stimuli it receives. No more, no less, although its response is greatly intricate.

Furthermore, even in the moronic rotifer as in the brain this modification is intelligent. It does tend to meet the conditions. The intelligence is not always infallible as respects any particular circumstances—sometimes the whole effort is a complete failure. But nevertheless it is an intelligent movement, not a blind groping: and in the vast majority of cases it is accurate.

I must not be understood as implying that this intelligence is a reasoned individual thing. It is sufficient to establish its presence in the situation. Intelligence is there. The law is ordered, rational, reciprocating. Indeed it is intelligent beyond the devisement of any individual human intelligence. We must try to examine later what it may be. But its presence in the compound is indubitable, just as the sensitive awareness-response is indubitable. That for the moment must suffice.

6

This collection of elements for discussion—rather than for thesis— is strengthened by a return up another branch of evolution to a consideration of the vegetable kingdom. Indubitably the most complex plant is higher in the scale of development than the simplest animal. The sage, with its complicated system of counter-poised levers, pivots and traps to assure cross-fertilization is an infinitely complex being as compared with the infusorians or the one-celled protozoa. Life here has followed a different branch of evolution.

To adduce many examples in plants of this sort of awareness-response, through an awareness-mechanism, to outside stimuli, in a manner to indicate the presence of intelligence, would consume too much space. The reader is advised to go to the library. A few examples must suffice here.

It must be noted, first of all, that the lowest forms of animal life are absolutely indistinguishable in characteristics and functions from the lowest forms of plant life.[8] 'The *englena* and *chlanydunonos*, for instance, behave almost exactly like protozoa, and are plants. Some forms are uncertain; no one knows whether they must be considered as plants or as animals.[9]

---

[8] Maeterlinck—The Intelligence of the Flowers in The Measure of the Hours; Farr, Plant Psychology in Atlantic Monthly, Dec. 1922; The Outline of Science; Herrick's Wonders of Plant Life; Muiler's Fertilization of Flowers will do to start on.

[9] The pedinella while floating nourishes itself in typical plant fashion: when fixed, by accidental running aground, it feeds as an animal on living organisms. See Appendix II.

Structurally, too, there is really no fundamental difference. Plants are cellular. The only difference, there, is that sometimes the plant-cells contain plastides, which manufacture food, and that their walls are so rigid that they prevent the formation or development of motor tissues. That is why plants cannot move about; why they cannot express themselves through motor activity. But they have definite sense-organs, some of them even more delicately responsive than man's; in their sieve tubes they possess as adequate nervous systems continuous vehicles of impulse from the smallest root tendrils to the tips of the leaves; they form and break habits;—in short, they exhibit all the elements of true consciousness according to our definition.

Prof. Clifford Farr collects so beautifully appropriate a series of examples of these basic similarities that it seems worthwhile to repeat them here, though in abridged form.

Man has his organ of equilibrium, which is a beautifully adjusted mechanism by which a declination from the vertical of a few degrees is detected and compensated. The plant possesses certain root cells at the bottom of which rest small loose grains. When by inclination of the plant these roll anywhere except where they belong—accurately on the bottom—a message is thereby sent to a motor organism which at once sets the plant vertical again. And thereby an inclination of a very small fraction of one degree is instantly detected and rectified. A man may be very considerably off-balance without becoming aware of it, but a plant cannot be pushed off its normal a fraction of an inch without being very much concerned about it.

The extreme sensitiveness to touch is so well known that it need only be mentioned here. The varieties of flowers that close up tight on the lightest contact, the rarer plants that seize their prey, the delicate gropings and withdrawings of tendrils are all well known. So too with sensitiveness to light. We are all informed as to how sunflowers and many other blooms turn toward the sun; we are familiar with the blossoms that go to sleep at nightfall and awaken at daybreak. The finer microscopic reactions to light are not so familiar but are much more wonderful. They fulfil many needs in the plant's life history, and demonstrate the possession of especial and delicate sense-organs by which the plant becomes aware.

Plants are more sensitive to pressure than we are; they are more sensitive to electrical stimuli. The weakest current we can become aware of amounts to about ten milliamperes: a plant's root exposed to one twenty-five-thousandth of a milliampere will indicate its awareness of that minute current by curving in the direction of the cathode.

It is a fact that in the human body there are cells more remote from a nerve than are any cells in a plant remote from its nerves—the sieve tubes.

These things, from one point of view, may be classed as "reflex actions" of course—if that helps any. We have, I hope, done something toward wiping out any basic distinction, as far as pure consciousness is concerned, between reflex action and any other action. But in its sensitiveness to light the plant may be shown to construct habits. In other words a psychic thing—a habit—may be shown capable of counteracting a "mechanical physical response." Place a marigold in darkness during the day, and expose it to illumination at night—a direct reversal of its usual life. In about a week's time it will have acquired a new habit of opening at night and closing during the day. But it will not do so within the first twenty-four hours, nor in forty-eight. Now by further experiment of the same sort it may gradually be induced to take on eight-hour shifts of opening and closing. But if the attempt is further pursued, and an effort is made to shorten the periods to four hours, then the marigold, as if in disgust, gives it all up and returns to its old twelve hour periods, irrespective of how you manipulate the lights. Here we come very close to placing plant consciousness within even the classic psychological definitions— though that, we must repeat, is not necessary for our thesis. Psychologists define consciousness as "emerging when reflex acts will not meet the needs of a situation." When we reverse the illumination, we have an instance of the reflex act not meeting the situation, for during the first night of illumination the petals remained closed. The plant has encountered a new situation, outside its own or its ancestor's experience, and it takes time for adjustment.

The deeper we delve into this most fascinating subject the more thoroughly are we convinced that we cannot deny the vegetable kingdom consciousness within the terms of our definition. It possesses awareness, through an awareness-mechanism. The fact that its mechanism has carried the stimulus is indicated by the fact of its response according to the laws of its individual being. The response is intelligent.

Nor must we too hastily deny the plant at least the rudiments of psychical consciousness in the narrower sense of the term. That consciousness is admittedly rudimentary as compared to man's, or the higher animals. But then the consciousness of Tony-in-the-ditch is admittedly rudimentary as compared with that of a great poet or a great musician or a great scientist. He is actually aware of an appallingly less number of things, and he is not so keenly aware of those things he knows.

Pleasure, in essence, is defined as a return to equilibrium, pain as a departure from equilibrium. If that is the case, the plant in its marvelous and delicate adjustments and compensations must feel pleasure and pain. Strike the leaf of a sensitive plant sharply and it will shrink away and curl up as though distressed; stroke it gently and it will curve upward to meet the finger. Fanciful perhaps: perhaps not.

7

Keeping in mind this successive diminution in degree, though not in kind; and applying the same criteria; let us go farther down the scale, on a sort of slumming trip as a cure for snobbishness. It is most important not to forget that we must anticipate a progressive simplification. If we go far enough we must not permit ourselves to expect more than a rudiment, a germ, a potentiality of what we find fully and elaborately exemplified further up. It has been so in our investigation of substance, where the two hundred and fifty thousand or so things which it is estimated our known cosmos contains have been gradually refined down to eighty-odd elements. When we say that a stone has consciousness, or a piece of iron, we do not need to endow it with all the *attributes* of consciousness that we find fully developed in a human being. That would be as absurd as to predicate of Tony-in-the-ditch a knowledge of astronomy.

Let us see what happens when a stone comes into relation with something outside itself. The alternating influences of frost, rain, and sun in turn exert themselves upon it. The rock splits.

We explain this phenomenon by ascribing it to "the action of natural law." Of course this is a correct statement as far as it goes. But what is that except another way of saying that certain ordered processes under the law have obtained from that stone a response, an indication of awareness, according to the mechanism of its very primitive being? The stone has become aware of the fact that it has been acted upon. How do we know that? Because it has split. The splitting is the manifestation of its awareness, its response to something outside itself.

Or if it objected that this is a negative yielding to force rather than a positive action,—as if one should push the stone, and ascribe its rolling to itself rather than to the push.—consider the recuperation of metal after fatigue. Iron under repeated stress becomes wearied, sometimes to the danger point of giving way entirely. But given a period free from stress and it recuperates, rehabilitates itself, becomes rested. It tends to recover its equilibrium; and in the process the microscopist of poetic vision might see the dulled, blind, painful gropings of a consciousness infinitely simple, torpid, frozen fast in the inert and stubborn material body of its manifestation—yet big with dreams.

Here once more we have a great simplicity as the result of our final analysis. We followed physical matter back until in its inceptions it had become so nearly a pure force that we could hardly define it in terms of matter at all. In the same fashion life stripped itself of its gay and lively attributes to emerge in a universal simplicity that must animate all things or they could not exist at all. Now consciousness also we find to be a requisite ingredient. A thing that should not respond in any manner to any law—were such a thing conceivable—would be indeed a "dead" thing, a thing without consciousness. Such is impossible.

8

It might be as well to digress at this point for a moment's glance at our own position in relation to all this. So tremendously complicated an arrangement of matter are we, as compared with the rest of the creation we know; so tremendously alive; so tremendously conscious, that we are inclined, unless we watch out, to overestimate ourselves, and to consider ourselves as about the most important criteria to which all other things must be referred. Unless we are exclusively occupied with a worm's eye view of ourselves, that is, as far as we are concerned, a correct enough attitude, up to a certain point and as a working hypothesis.

But certainly as far as physical matter is concerned, and probably— by analogy—as far as life and consciousness go, we occupy as yet a rather low point. Down the scale through the element, the molecule, the atom, the electron; through man, beast, bird, plant, protozoa, and the geological constituents; through all the grades of consciousness from a Newton to the dull slow stirrings of mechanical reaction, is a long, long road; but we can see all the distance, retrace practically all the steps. Casting outward, however, we see only the beginning, and a small beginning at that. At a certain point the mind begins to lose the value of its figures; yet the figures lead unwaveringly on.

Our insignificance in the physical universe we have begun to realize. The facts can be piled up until they cease to register. For instance, if we will use our imagination to reduce the magnitude of the earth to that of a pinhead,—we remaining the same size as now—then the sun becomes the size of an orange and is thirty feet away, and Neptune on the outskirts of our solar system resembles a pea and is a thousand feet distant. Remember that man inhabits the pinhead. That is for our solar system alone. But our solar system is not alone: it has neighbors. The nearest of these is the star, Alpha Centauri. It would be, in the shrunk universe we have imagined, roughly thirteen million feet from the orange that represented the sun! And that is our very next neighbor.

When we begin to measure farther, we have to abandon[10] our tidy little standards and adopt new ones. Light, we know, travels at the terrific rate of 186,000 miles a second. In calculating distances between stars astronomers adopt this as a unit. It is now estimated that there are something near fifty billion of stars (*sic*) in our universe, and that light—travelling at 186,000 miles a second—would take about fifty thousand years to traverse it from end to end! Furthermore it is now practically certain that there are other universes beside our own, some of them visible as nebule. There would seem to be plenty of room!

From such considerations it becomes at once very evident that, in spite of the enormous discrepancy in the scale between ourselves and the microscopic, We occupy a pretty low position in the whole scheme of space. In order to bring atoms and electrons into a size that can be handled we need only to reduce our own size ten billion times.[11] Then the atoms would seem to us about three feet in diameter and the electrons about the size of a pinpoint. Of course a ten-billionth reduction somewhat staggers the imagination; but is nothing at all as compared to fifty thousand years of steady travelling at the rate of nearly sixty-seven million miles an hour!

These figures and pictures are not introduced to dazzle or confuse. They are intended merely to show that as far as the material is concerned we are by no means the last word in possibility, nor in probability. Just at the moment we happen to bear a relation of about fourteen million steps to the diameter of the thing we live on. A shift in that proportion— up or down; or a shift of that proportion to some other thing to live on, and we would possess an entire new relationship and perspective. There seems not only to be plenty of space but plenty of possibilities!

It is in my opinion not at all improbable that the same considerations affect the other two members of what appears to be an indissolvable

---

[10] Or what is the same thing, increasing our own size proportionally.

[11] Leaving, of course, the rest of the physical universe as it is.

and independent trinity. Life and consciousness seem to possess at least the potentiality, if not the actuality, of similar shifts of scale and relationship. We are not aware of higher forms of consciousness than our own, as we are aware of the greater standards of space than our own, but that is not conclusive evidence of their non-existence. Or, if they do not yet exist, is our own present self-gratulating estate any evidence that consciousness is not capable of development infinitely beyond its embodiment in ourselves of today?

9

That is, however, a matter for more consideration in its proper place. For the moment it is sufficient that we find ourselves in possession of a completed circle. Any material substance *must* possess life: segregate life must possess the power of reaction to outside stimulus; as consciousness reduces itself finally to awareness-response, all life must have consciousness. All things in time and space—within, it must be remembered, the widest limit markers we have set to our understanding—must be material, must be alive, must be conscious.

That is as far out and out—and in and in—as our vision and knowledge can take us. But does not this convergence justify us in extending our straight lines to a common meeting point? We have found all matter to be finally one thing. We have determined life to be primordially one thing. We have reasoned that consciousness, however widely it seems to vary in degree, must ultimately define itself as one thing. Within our time and space limit markers we have found matter, however tenuous; life, however sluggish; consciousness, however simple, to be omnipresent. Does not this more than suggest that they themselves are ultimately, although in some manner outside our markers, also one thing? that life, consciousness, matter are manifestations of a single quality?

How this can be we are not capable of understanding, any more than we are capable of understanding how there can be no end to space or time. But we are capable of taking the abstract conception as a working hypothesis and examining how the accepted facts of life fit with it or are explained by it.

CHAPTER 4

LIFE, CONSCIOUSNESS, AND MATTER

~

1

L IFE, consciousness, and matter we should find then to be in essence expressible one in terms of the other. This proves to be the case. Matter, when we speak of it in its electronic aspects, is defined as a balance and interplay of vital forces. It is defined by some philosophers as a state of consciousness. It may be measured and weighed and evaluated, of course, strictly according to its own attributes. Similarly life has been philosophically stated in terms of pure consciousness; and mechanistic science has never given over the attempt to reduce it to a purely material concept. The same can be said of consciousness. All these points of view are true, but only partially so. The mistake is in too great a rigidity; in an insistence that because one can define the other in its own terms, therefore the other cannot exist. Instead of seeing the underlying unity, the specialist is convinced that all but his specialty is phantasmagoric.

This is interesting; but it is after all not of the least importance. The specialist must wear blinders in order to travel his straight road. What is important is this: that not only may life, consciousness and matter be defined in terms of one another, but they manifest themselves in one another.

This is worth pausing over, for it is a fundamental. Though a basic unity lies outside the limit markers of our complete understanding—and as we have seen in the last chapter there is an almost overwhelming probability of such a unity—within our three-dimensioned space and our three-dimensioned time we have to deal with a trinity.[1] At the point of their completest simplicity they almost merge; but at the moment with which we wish to deal with them they are clearly enough defined. We cannot remain forever at fundamental simplicities—not if we are to formulate a satisfactory daily companion of belief. The members of this trinity, to repeat, are constantly manifesting themselves in one another.

Life clothes itself in matter to form the varied physical world: consciousness seems to order and make intelligent and understandable both the processes and forms of life; matter reaches the potentialities of its substance through the life and consciousness which it embodies. They interact mutually.

But for the purposes of our examination we may reduce this trinity to a duality. In the mathematics of the universe threes and twos seem to be especially favored. The two members of the duality appear to correspond to the great complementary opposition that obtains all through nature—male and female, positive and negative, the plus and minus of chemistry, active and passive. We have substance, which embodies, on the one side; and life and consciousness, which manifest themselves, on the other. Substance furnishes the material, consciousness and life the intention or idea and the vital force of achievement.

2

This is a logical enough supposition, and will be and has been accepted by a great many people without the necessity of further argument and demonstration. However, it will be more satisfactory to inquire whether we have any actual knowledge to sustain the view. Let us

---

[1] I have been asked why an underlying unity is necessary or desirable, why a nature may not be conceived as flatly and finally dual or triune, why it is necessary to suppose final intelligence. The answer is purely logical. We must postulate an inunderstandable infinity, for the simple reason adduced that, like the child looking at the sky, we can conceive of no end to space—or time. But if there is infinity, then it must include everything that is. Otherwise it would not be infinity. It would be all things and all space except the thing it did not include, which would be outside of it, on the other side of the wall. Therefore, since there is such a thing as intelligence matter, and life, and consciousness, the finite must be postulated as intelligent, etc. These things are in last analysis its attributes.

concentrate for the purpose of discussion on one phase of this mutual interaction.

A tree is a material thing, composed of cells of different kinds and in certain arrangements.

These cells, in turn, are made up of molecules and atoms of various elements, which of course are merely arrangements of electrons. Why do these things, at this place, arrange themselves in the form of a tree, while identically the same sort of things arrange themselves over there in the form of a butterfly?

That would seem to be a simple enough question. It has been variously answered; but in analysis the answers prove merely to push the question farther back. "Action of natural law," says one. What then causes one kind of law to act here to produce the tree and another kind to act there to produce the butterfly? "That is a result of evolution," is the answer; and for years we are lost in the delightful by-paths of evolutionary process, from which we emerge at last with a fairly clear conception of growth, to be sure, but with no adequate explanation. We prove that evolution is a fact. The spontaneous appearance of forms superior to the originals seems logically to be a scientific and philosophical impossibility. Yet we have proved mutations, abrupt transformism, certain aspects of the acquisition of instincts. Especially mutation—or the abrupt appearance of new clearly differentiated forms of life.[2] The slow experiments and careful reasoning of years has led us to the point where we can clearly see that while evolution itself is fundamental, many of the processes of evolution are as yet obscure. Nature herself, in insect transformation, presents to us an amazing example. -In its life history the very butterfly of which we are speaking upsets the old classical theories of an unbroken material progression through environmental influences solely; and forces us to introduce some new and vital factor of growth.

3

So significant is this signpost set by Nature to guide us, that it will be worthwhile to consider it in detail.

We have long been accustomed to trace what seemed to the scientists of another generation the course of evolution through a supposedly

---

[2] The subject is too long for detailed discussion. It is now of historical value only, as the conclusions are about out of the controversial stage. Le Dantec, De Vries, Blaringham, Cope, Geley may be consulted in any good library.

unbroken series of development. It was presumed that one form must necessarily evolve from the next one lower. When gaps occurred in the even gradations and mergings, it was assumed that the forms representing them had been destroyed so completely as to leave no trace. They were "missing links," whose remains might one day be discovered. Moreover, the mergings were held to be gradual, and the modifications solely due to the influence of such things as environment and the struggle for existence. On the basis of this supposition scientific thought tried to explain evolution on the single basis of matter, and to define the individual thing as a mere cellular complex.

But proved mutations, both in fossil forms and in species now living, threw this entire conception into confusion. New species sometimes appear abruptly, without transitional forms.[3] Natural selection, the struggle for existence, and the other classical factors are strongly contributing, but they are not first causes. Even the idea that new forms take shape as the direct result of environment is open to grave doubt, though the new form is indubitably expressly fitted to the environment. It begins to seem that the new form is not molded by the environment as a sculptor models a plastic figure. Rather it is first foreshadowed, then constructed by something within, which sees a need and answers it.

A moment's thought, even without reference to the accumulation of scientific evidence, will show the reasonableness of this view. The classic idea had it that improvement, appearing by chance, so to speak, in an individual gave him an advantage over other individuals which enabled him to survive where others perished. The transmission by heredity of the improvement established the modification and eventually led to an ascending evolution of species. That is the simplest statement of the pure Darwinian idea of the method of evolution.

The modifying reasoning can be stated as simply, though it, too, has a library of proof and discussion back of it. Geley puts it into a short paragraph.

"In order that any given modification occurring in the characteristics of a species or of an individual, should give to that species or to that individual an appreciable advantage in the struggle for life, it is evident that *this modification must be sufficiently marked to be utilizable.*"

But a new organ or a new faculty is never so. It is adumbrated in embryo, and develops only very slowly. Conceivably the development of wings gave the flying reptile an advantage over his pedestrian

---

[3] The evening primrose among plants, and the fruit fly among animals are present day examples of mutation.

cousin—after he got them so he could fly with them. Embryonic wings appearing by hazard could give him no such advantage. The possessor would stand no more chance of surviving, and passing on his fortuitous acquisition, than any of his fellows.

So evident did this become that naturalists soon modified their ideas to include what might be called, not natural, but organic selection. This hypothesis laid the stress on pressure of environment. It is not chance that produces the modification, but necessity. The development of new organs or characteristics comes from their repeated use, and their atrophy from neglect. These adaptations are at first very slight, but are emphasized by use until they result in major transformations. This is the simplest possible statement of the Lamarckian theory, and is still held by many who seek to reduce their science to the terms of one substance.

At first glance it seems to be a more intellectually satisfying doctrine. It explains much that pure Darwinism fails to meet. But it too falls short of accounting for mutation, and for such phenomena as the transition from a water life to a land life, or of a land life to an air life. That these transitions are due to the pressure of some sort of necessity there can be no doubt—whether the necessity was physical, as of overcrowding or deadly pursuit, or some urge of development. But the idea that they are due to adaptation is untenable.

"The ancestral species, adapted to very special surroundings, had no need to change them, and had they felt the need, would have been unable to meet it. How could the reptilian ancestor of the bird adapt itself to surroundings which were not its own and could only become its own *after* it had passed from the reptilian to the bird form? ... There is no connection between the biology of the larva, which represents, to some degree at any rate, the primitive state of the ancestral insect, and the biology of the perfect insect form. One cannot even conceive by what mysterious series of adaptations, an insect, accustomed to life underground or in water could succeed in gradually creating for itself wings for an aerial life, closed to it and doubtless unknown.

"When, further, one considers that this mysterious series of adaptations would have to take place, not once, by a kind of 'natural miracle,' but as many times as there are genera of insects,—" then the case becomes hopeless.

"Adaptations," concludes Geley, "appear as a consequence, sometimes as a determining factor, but never as a sufficient and essential cause."[4]

---

[4] See also Arthur Thomson for an admirable discussion of the difference between a modification and a mutation—Outline of Science.

In other words, according to this concept, evolution has come about not so much by the action of environment as in conformity to it. The developing organism in some mysterious fashion feels its need in correspondence, and at once begins to take steps toward meeting that need. The modification is sometimes long foreshadowed, is long in preparation, remains long in unusable form, long has itself no influence on the organism's chances of survival or predominance over its fellows. Development is by the idea from within.

4

This hypothesis receives enormous strength when one considers embryonic development and histolysis.

The progress of the embryo, as is well known, more or less completely sums up the physiological history of the organism. The baby passes rapidly from the simple cell through all intermediate stages to the human. At one period he has the gill clefts of fishes, at another he resembles the embryo turtle in the structure of his heart, his first trace of a backbone is the notochord of the lamprey, and soon. Any organism assumes successive forms, quite different one from the other, before reaching its final stage. The tadpole has all the characteristics of organs and method of a fish. Suddenly, without any change in surroundings or life, it develops legs, lungs, and a three chambered heart, and becomes a frog. It is impossible to ascribe these changes to a change in chemical equilibrium, as mechanistic science would have it, without the aid of the directing idea. Concede, for the purposes of argument only, that this might have been the case in the countless years of the development of the species, that slowly there did take place, in response to environment, chemical changes that modified structure. How about the individual? What causes in him these chemical changes? Not environment, surely; but some inner principle inherent in the individual germ from which he sprang, some stored and specific idea compressed into the compass of a single plasm.

But if this is not conclusive, consider the insect. Throughout the development of the ordinary embryo, however rapidly it takes place, we can trace a continuity. One form follows another. They join hands, so to speak. The elementary expands to the simple; the simple to the varied; the varied to the complex. Each idea, progressively elaborate, builds itself in the progressively elaborate material prepared for it. In the insect, however, we find a definite break, when the old idea is discarded, the old substance melted down into primordial substance, and a new idea manifested in the raw material.

This takes place in the chrysalis. We are all familiar with the externals of the operation. The caterpillar, after leading a pedestrian and assimilative life, constructs himself an impervious shell; after a period he comes forth as a butterfly. It remained for Weissman to point our way to finding out what happened inside that chrysalis. The body of the insect is dematerialized, melted down. It is completely disintegrated, liquefied. It becomes a single substance from which specific distinctions and organs presently disappear. From that raw material a new kind of creature is formed. It feeds differently, it leads a different life, it has different organs and functions. This new creature's new organs are not extensions of or modifications of the organs and functions of the old creature. They seem in no way to have any affiliation with the destroyed organs. They are different.

Of course this is no more remarkable than that the individual human cell should possess, packed away in its tiny compass, all the potentialities of the varied and complicated organs and functions of the adult body. But it is more direct and striking. Here we have before our eyes a complete organization dissolved back to its original plastic material, and in that material a new idea of the creature manifested. It is, as we have said, almost as though this example, at once so unique and so arresting, had been placed as a guidepost to our thought.

5

The invariable presence of the idea, or Intention, or whatever we please to call it—the conditioning central dynamism that expresses itself in the material—becomes also evident in other departments besides the zoological, once the principle is grasped. It is only recently that chemistry has realized that there is an unexplained force or power involved in its own reactions. Two parts of hydrogen do not combine with one part of oxygen without the demonstration—and hence the presence of a third thing, an unknown X. This X may as easily be defined in terms of the intention as of force.

Consider a man in the process of doing any piece of work. He utilizes energy. Not one infinitesimal fraction of an ounce of it did he produce. It has been there all the time. But he segregates it, and he directs it into channels. From the reservoir he dips some up in his own cup and by use makes it his own. He *intentions* it. And when he so intentions it, he does not make any more nor any less: he merely changes the adjustment. And until he intentions it, it is merely existent. We can thus, in the case of the human being, see very clearly that a thing is created, in the sense of being embodied or manifested, solely by the idea or intention put into it. We have also seen, though perhaps more dimly, that in the department of zoology the raw material—as in the chrysalis—takes its shape in conformity to an idea of the thing, or an intention.

Nor does this reasoning fail in the lower organizations. It too simplifies, just as we found life and consciousness to simplify; but in essence it remains the same.

Salt is composed of chlorine and sodium. Now the mere presence of quantities of chlorine and quantities of sodium does not mean that all will combine to produce salt. Only an exact proportion will do so. When we understand what they are, we can produce them, and make a definite quantity of salt; and we can make it because we intend to make it. And when all is said and done the formula for salt is not merely sodium *plus* chlorine *equals* salt. It is sodium, *plus* chlorine, plus the thing that happens when they get together, equals salt.

Now it cannot conceivably matter one bit whether the combination is effected deliberately by man or "in the course of nature." The process is the same and the formula is the same. The chemist apprehends and deliberately uses the *idea* of salt; but the idea is there. He doesn't change it nor add to it. He merely makes it personal by intending it. He cannot produce his result without the idea. Furthermore, he did not originate the idea. If he had never discovered how to make salt, salt nevertheless would have been in existence. Here again we cannot avoid recognizing the presence, as an ingredient, of intelligence. The making of things is intelligent. There are definite ideas, which are embodied. It is useless to look at it from another angle and to attempt to ascribe it all to the "workings of natural law," and to rest on that statement. The natural law is intelligent. We find it so, and in complete reliance on that fact we utilize it. If it were not intelligent our own intelligence could not so utilize it. Turn and twist it as we will, the Idea is there, embodying itself in the fashion that expresses it best.

6

Nor does it matter from which aspect we view it. We have still our trinity of attributes of the underlying unity expressing itself interchangeably. Substance, the material of embodiment; life, the force or dynamism;

consciousness, the guardian of the idea. In this mutual interaction they assist each other upward in the spiral of evolution. Through successive: utilizations by life and consciousness substance becomes increasingly complex in structure, increasingly responsive, varied and plastic and therefore increasingly capable of representing. Through successive embodiments in substance life emerges from the dull torpidity that binds it in the iron to the vibrant flashing animation of its highest present development. By means of successive demonstrations in substance and experiments in life, consciousness extends and elaborates and perfects its ideas.

CHAPTER 5

HUMAN-NESS, TREE-NESS, AND DOG-NESS

~

1

IN the last chapter we have instanced certain phenomena which are, each in its way, examples of mutual interaction between consciousness, life, and substance, which seem at once equal and universal. We have seen from them, and from the inexorable logic behind them, that any manifestation whatever is both preceded by and governed by the *idea* of that manifestation. And since consciousness in its finite aspect as one of a trinity is the guardian of the Idea, it is the governing factor in that trinity. Furthermore, we have seen that in *essence* consciousness is a single sort of thing; life is a single sort of thing; also substance. This is so in spite of the immense variety of manifestations of each.

Since consciousness is the governing factor, manifesting its idea in substance, by means of the force of life, it is evident that our chief concern, when it comes to a question of orienting ourselves, must be with consciousness, rather than with substance. Life we ally with consciousness. We must examine the cosmos and our place in it from that angle.

That attitude, then, to repeat, shows us consciousness manifesting itself in substance by means of life. Life exhibits many and varied forms; and these forms are fashioned each according to its own idea or plan. It does not require a very great stretching of the spirit or extension of vision to see this, at least as a picture. Especially this fact is borne home to one who contemplates the springtime. The green living things, the trees and bushes and grasses and bright flowers; the birds, the little animals, the myriad insects; all seem to be in essential, not differing and distinct phenomena, but an upsurgence of a single vitality seeking outlet. It is as though a fountain of inexhaustible energy were throwing upward a ceaseless spray of living things. Were we able by some juggling of our time ratios apparently to speed up the earth rotation as related to ourselves, so that the seasons would pass before us as minutes and seconds instead of years, this rhythmic surge of life would become more vividly apparent. The lift and fall of individual existences would be like drops in the fountain's jet. Nothing seems to us more peacefully satisfying in its dignity of permanence than a forest of great trees, yet it is conceivable that under a changed time ratio to the beholder it would appear to spring from the soil into the rounded soft mobility and to sink back into the soil again as briefly and as gracefully as rises and falls a wave on the sea.

This is all very well as a generality. The picture is an inspiring one. But it satisfies only as long as we stand apart watching our hypothetically speeded-up world. When we reenter our own time ratio we are struck not only by the abundance of life's overflow, but by its amazing variety of forms. A single cubic foot of the earth's surface will reveal to the microscope a staggeringly numerous population going about its lawful occasions. Any flower garden of a warm and sunny afternoon will display apparently enough of a variety of life forms to answer any conceivable needs of correspondence to environment; and yet outside the plot are more and more and yet more. The trees of the forest stand thick and dense, and clothe well the hills. The pines live on the rocky highlands or in the sandy soil, and the broad-leaved trees on the rounded hills or in the fertile valley. But they are not merely pines and broadleaves. There are white pines, and sugar pines, and yellow pines, and Norway pines, and the various firs, and the hemlocks and larches and dozens more. And there is birch and elm, maple and hickory and beech and cottonwood and a host of species beside. How does it happen that life manifests itself so variously, that consciousness has so many ideas? Why in the universal substance, animated by the universal life, does consciousness embody here the idea of a dog, there of a tree, yonder of a human being?

2

To make even a beginning of understanding we must recognize that consciousness itself must, at this present moment in which we live, be differentiated into many qualities. There is a certain type or kind or quality of consciousness possessed by a dog, and another type or kind or quality of consciousness possessed by a man. They differ one from the other. There is still another type or kind or quality of consciousness possessed by a tree; and that, of course, differs from the other two. We might say of consciousness in general that sometimes it has a dog-ness, sometimes a tree-ness, sometimes a human-ness. In other words, though consciousness is in essence a single sort of thing, it possesses, or has developed, different qualities.

It is the manifesting in life and substance of these differing qualities of consciousness that makes the variety that has so amazed us.

There is nothing new or startling in this proposition. We have seen in the previous chapter the same truth expressed from a physiological point of view when we considered the transformations that take place in the embryo and in the chrysalis. The complete idea of the adult organism has at first been compressed into a single germ cell, in the one case, and in the liquefied raw material of a disintegrated old form in the other. The idea in both cases was the idea of that particular quality of consciousness. The baby-ness was inherent in the germ cell: the butterfly-ness in the chrysalis. In other words, the differing *quality of consciousness* in each case made the difference in the form of life. It is that which makes it a bit of separateness from all other consciousness; which makes it aware; which makes it what it is; which picks it forth from the in understandable cosmic consciousness. It is this, rather than a literal Platonic "prototype," which determines species and kinds.

Nevertheless, we must beware of conceiving of these qualities apart from the consciousness of which they are phases or attributes.

3

Let us concentrate, now, for the purpose of discussion, on a single quality of consciousness.

We will take, for convenience, the tree quality, which we have called tree-ness. That tree-ness tends to express or embody itself in substance; or it tends to make individual the life force in substance—whichever you will. The result is finally a tree, as we know it. That tree is an organism of well-known form. The form is determined by the environment. It takes shape on a globe with certain physical characteristics of size, soil, atmosphere, moisture and heat. Its own size, its organs, its functioning, its shape and appearance are all conditioned by these facts. In other words, in the environment we know, Tree-ness manifests itself as a thing not over three or four hundred feet tall nor over thirty feet thick, with woody fiber for stability and the necessary circulation of its sap; in branching form for the accommodation of its foliation; in the foliation for those functions of breathing and absorption which life in an atmosphere of hydrogen and oxygen makes necessary; and so on. The result of these, and other, correspondences, as a whole, is the tree as we see it.

But now conceive in imagination the quality of tree-ness manifesting itself in matter wherein relationships differ widely from those found on our earth. I think it a not unfair assumption that the quality of consciousness* which we have called "tree-ness,"—or indeed any other quality of consciousness—may quite well exist elsewhere in the finite cosmos than on our somewhat insignificant earth. Indeed, philosophically, one can go farther and predicate that in infinite consciousness all qualities of consciousness must exist everywhere. That for the moment does not concern us.[1] What we are interested in is the thought that the tree quality almost certainly must manifest itself elsewhere than on our earth; and that it must almost certainly embody itself in matter whose physical relationships are different from our own.

The atmosphere may be lighter or heavier or may lack entirely; the density of matter may be quite different; the temperatures may be far above or far below what we know. In short there may be a set of conditions so widely at variance with our own that no life as we know it could possibly sustain itself. On this account it has been the invariable speculative habit to state baldly and categorically that "life is obviously impossible on this, that, or the other planet or star or satellite because conditions there found are incapable of sustaining life."

This is, in my opinion, an obvious non-sequitur. Life in the forms we know may be obviously impossible. An air breathing animal cannot exist without air. But this by no means makes impossible the presence not only of life, but of the same qualities[2] of consciousness with which we

---

[1] Or the Idea of the tree.

[2] Dr, Levi Noble in his studies of volcanoes found alge living in a temperature of 200° F. The adaptation had taken place, although this degree of heat had been supposed to be fatal to all life.

are familiar. They would, through the necessity of physical maintenance, embody themselves in totally different forms with totally different functions, but they would express nevertheless the same qualities of consciousness, the same ideas.

Tree-ness might manifest itself in the material environment of some distant solar system—that of Canopus for instance,—where the predominating elements of matter are not only new and strange, but which bear to each other relations cast in a novel numerical ratio. Here the tree quality would not, in the construction of its functioning body, deal with hydrogen and oxygen or the chemical formulae of moisture and air and soil, nor with heat as we know it. For these familiar correspondences other correspondences are substituted. But—and this is important—these new correspondences do provide for exactly the same satisfactions of the same basic needs.

I do not know what the basic needs of the tree quality of consciousness may be, but let us name stability as one of them, and let us assume that a rooted stalk of woody fiber is the physical mechanism by which that need expresses itself. Both these assumptions are quite gratuitous, and adopted merely for the purpose of discussion. It is conceivable that in our Canopus solar system the attribute of stability will be better expressed by an equilibrium of gases, and that the other attributes of the tree quality—whatever they may be, *but which in their sum total make up tree-ness*—can find each its mechanism of expression in the same medium. Then, obviously, we would have something that to our earth eyes would not in the slightest degree resemble a tree. Nevertheless, *considered as a reality*,[3] and not as an appearance, it would be a tree. All the attributes of tree-ness would be physically expressed.

Of course I realize the force of the argument that possibly the tree quality would find expression only in an environment that duplicates or nearly duplicates our own, and that therefore the only embodiment of tree-ness must be in the form we know. That is possible. But it seems to me to arrogate to our own especial conditions an importance which our position in the spatial cosmos hardly seems to warrant. That any quality of consciousness, however relatively unimportant, should find itself confined to such a pin point in the starry heavens borders somewhat on the absurd.

All this is merely a game of "supposing." The decision of the question outlined above is not at this time intrinsically important. Its suggestion

---

[3] i.e., the expression in some kind of substance of the basic realities of certain ideas.

is intended as another stretching exercise; just as was the consideration of the size of our known universe. There is plenty of room: there is also plenty of possibility.

4

In the preceding section we touched lightly upon a rather abstruse conception. It is necessary now to consider it more clearly before we can go on to speculate on our old question of why the tree quality manifests at this point in space rather than that, or the dog quality in that rather than this.

If we get clearly in mind differing and varied qualities of consciousness expressing themselves in physical form, we are likely to form a mental image of a sort of series of separated reservoirs or pools or vague storage bodies of some sort, each representing one or another quality of consciousness from which individual manifestations are drawn, so to speak. The temptation to visualize such a picture is almost irresistible. To avoid it we must go back to our first conception of infinite unity. In that aspect consciousness must be all one. It differentiates into qualities. But that differentiation is analogous, must be, to the manifestation of the human mind in anger, love, discrimination, speculation or the like. The mind does not divide itself off into separate compartments. This is only an analogy, for these aspects of the mind are powers and attributes, rather than qualities; but the point is well enough illustrated; and that is, that all qualities of consciousness exist potentially in every speck of consciousness.

It is only another way of saying what has many times been expressed theoretically by philosophers and fancifully by poets. Everything that is, is in everything that is. The "flower in the crannied wall" has bloomed for all the great seers. It is again, on the side of consciousness, the truth we have examined in the case of physical substance; when we found that proton and electron are in everything that is, and are always the same.

The conception, as we have said, is a little abstruse. If it prove a stumbling block it may be set one side. The alternative conception is not antagonistic to the main theme. The qualities of consciousness—the guardians of the idea back of every created thing (*sic*)—may be looked upon as separate reservoirs from which the individual is drawn, so to speak. But all analogy in other fields inclines me personally to the view that, though the qualities of consciousness must be distinct, each in itself, a complete whole containing all its own elements, those qualities are so interfused throughout all cosmos that we may literally say that each point of space contains in itself all the elements of them all. In the all-pervasive cosmic consciousness,—which, we must reiterate, is akin to the all-pervasive ether of substance, or vitality of force,—complete tree-ness, complete dog-ness, complete human-ness, complete anything-ness, up to the point of present development of consciousness, exist everywhere in suspension, as it were, ready to precipitate when the conditions of their being are fulfilled. Given the complicated conditions favorable to the tree quality of consciousness, we have the tree. In other words, the reason why at any particular point in space we have a tree rather than an ant or a starfish or a dog or an antelope or a bed of moss is, not that the tree quality is stronger at that point, but because the conditions for trees are stronger at that point.

5

That is so simple as to be self-evident. If we stop there, we can flatter ourselves that we rest on an axiom. But the rest is very brief. As soon as we have caught our breath we must get up and go on. Why, at that particular point, do one set of conditions obtain rather than another? Why at point A are the conditions all assembled for the production of a tree, and at point B for a sunflower? Is it pure chance? Is it the balanced interplay of many forces? If the latter, how does that come about?

If we are content to think we have explained things when we name them—as most of us are,—we say the conditions are the result of a long evolution working itself out. We begin with the stardust in the void, and we trace through planetary evolution the formation and cooling of worlds, the carving of continents, the births and deaths of millions of entities of rock and mold, the modifying influences of waters and ices and the upheaval of mountains and the fierceness of suns and the soothing of the cooling mists and the watering of rains. All these mighty influences have worked together until at one tiny spot everything is just right. Then one seed, out of thousands that have fallen on barren soil, germinates because at last the conditions are gathered. And we point out that these final conditions could be collected only because of a myriad of other phenomena, each of which required its own conditions which, in turn, were dependent on an equally complicated ancestry. The thing worked automatically, like a huge and infinitely complex machine. It is, again, a "product of natural law."

That is a good answer, as far as it goes; and serves to define for us our next question. What is this law? What is any law?

The first thing we notice, when we come to think the matter over, is that law, too, is a developing thing. Matter, life and consciousness may hold primordially in themselves all the possibilities they are slowly bringing out by evolution, but only as potentialities. They do not exist as active and concrete things until they are developed. So all law, on its potential side, undoubtedly exists; but it, too, most certainly does not become a *thing* until it acts. It starts from the very simple and works out into the complex. In essence it is one thing, just as we found all stuff is one stuff. Stuff is only our name for an actuality as is law. There is really nothing fixed or static about it, except in its inner essence. We actually know very little about it, except that our observation shows it to be harmonious and self-consistent. It appears to be working toward something; but we do not know its goal. We cannot even understand why there should be a goal. We do perceive, somewhat dimly to be sure, that in nature it seems to be tending toward two things—self-knowledge, and self-control. All steps in evolution contribute toward fitting the creature better to understand its own functions and correspondences to its environment, and by that understanding to get on better with its surroundings. We also perceive, when we look somewhat deeper, that there appears to be almost a passion for organization, and for a unity of direction under a diversity of forms. That is about all we are now able to know of law in itself.

But we can look a little deeper into how law works. To begin with, no one ever makes a law work, in the sense of a direct control. He merely assembles in proper juxtaposition and proportion the necessary conditions. Note that this is the same prerequisite to the manifestation in specific form of any quality of consciousness. Having done this much, he cannot prevent the law from working. We talk of lighting a fire as though we had actually created something out of a void. As a matter of fact we pile our wood, we place our kindling and our paper, we supply certain chemicals under motion and abrasion. The law steps in. Briefly expressed, we had an idea in our consciousness and manifested it in substance. There is no working of any law unless the conditions for that law are arranged.

How are they arranged? In the case of the fire we conceived the idea of the fire, and its desirability, and we knew the necessary things to do, and we did them. Briefly expressed, we felt a desire and we used our intelligence. In the case of the tree the necessary conditions that permitted—or forced—the law of its being to act were assembled by a great number of contributing causes. The soil was right because the conditions for the action of the laws that produce loam and humus had been collected and those laws had acted. The moisture was right because the conditions for the action of the laws that produce rainfall had been collected. And so on. The thing has been automatic, machine made. In all the complicated interplay one set of conditions depends upon and is the result of an antecedent set of conditions, which in turn have sprung from others. It seems in quite different case from our act of deliberate intelligence in assembling the fire conditions.

Is it? We have pushed the question back and back, but have we altered either its form or its importance? How do all these complicated dependencies come about? Through the law of evolution, the laws of interplay by which forces strain and pull and twist against each other, the law of increasing complexity, the law of progress—call it what you will. But it, in turn, is a law. It is an embracive law, but it seems to be just as definitely a law as that which caused the rain to fall on the seed. If it is a law, it—like all the other laws—must act because the conditions for its acting have been collected.

So, no matter how far back we go, sooner or later we must inevitably come to the same elements that laid our fire—desire and intelligence.

And here, once more, we find ourselves for the moment at the limits of our field. We can go back only so far without confusion. No matter how careful our analysis, we come at last to a point where we must stop to ask ourselves the old questions: what causes that in turn? why? And we find ourselves once more compelled to set workable limits inside the infinity of space and time, which we cannot understand.

From time to time we extend those limits. As we require more of space for our astronomical balances, more of time for our evolutionary perspectives, we reach out and appropriate what we need. But always beyond is the Unknown from which deliberately we veil the eyes of our understanding.

In like manner we reach back and back in appropriation of what we need in the beginnings of life and energy and consciousness. And always behind is the ultimate Inunderstandable which we cannot touch. We name it Spirit, the Thing Beyond, the Ultimate, God. And having planted our marker at the utmost point of the usable, we turn back to till our chosen field.

CHAPTER 6

ME-NESS

~

1

IT is one thing to say that all created things are manifestations or embodiments of consciousness; and quite another to predicate a distinct and individual consciousness within that quality for each and every one of these separate things. Whereabouts does the individual, as a separate thing, begin? How, theoretically, can we conceive of its originating?

We must here, of course, enter the realms of pure speculation, and if we are to speculate with any reasonable satisfaction we must have something to go by. It is an appropriate time to repeat that this is only an attempt to tell how at this time things seem to me, or seem reasonable to me. It is not an argument nor an effort at proselyting. The thing I would go by here is analogy. Analogies, if closely enough drawn, are a good basis for speculative hypothesis, for correct analogy is merely the same law working in two different mediums. If it works along certain general lines in the one substance, it is only logical to suppose that it will work along the same general lines in another.

Let us then drop back in pure theory to the very smallest and finest division of things of which we are capable, to a hypothetical mathematical point differentiated in infinite consciousness. It is like going back in substance to our electron, which means nothing unless in certain motions and juxtapositions. This point in consciousness is not doing anything, nor is it going anywhere. It just is. Introduced next into this almost total vacuum of consciousness the simplest possible intention, or idea, or direction. Direction, at this simplest, is represented by a line pointing from somewhere to somewhere else. That must give us at least two points. These might be so close to each other that they might seem to be superimposed: nevertheless, the moment we have two of them we have direction. And in order to get direction—which is the simplest idea of which consciousness is capable—we must have two points. This process is in almost exact analogy to the like process in the realm of substance where the simplest first expression is that of the single electron in opposition to the single proton.

But direction, or two points however close together, cannot be conceived apart from the time, however brief, it would take to get from one point to the other; nor of the space, however minute, between them. In other words, consciousness as a single unit—which can be, of course, only the infinite consciousness—can have neither time nor space nor motion. Only when there is a differentiation, when there are two points, does the idea of time,—and hence space and motion,—come in.

Our hypothetical little composite unit with only two things in it is very simple. Not much can be expressed by it in the way of idea or intention. Its functions in such expression must necessarily be extraordinarily limited. To accomplish anything further a third unit must be added, and to one side. Then we have the idea of the triangle, and of energy working not in a single line of direction, but of two— straight ahead and to one side. Here we enter plane geometry. The possibilities are many more than double those of two points, but they are still very limited. So let us add more points of consciousness; thus producing not only length and breadth, but thickness, and the more complex motion that must result from several forces exerting themselves in different directions. Sometimes this exertion is with one another, sometimes against.

This is mathematics, or mechanics, if one pleases; but it is also consciousness. And it is the remote inception of what we call intelligence, in that when reduced to its beginnings,—as we reduce substance to its electronic beginnings,—intelligence is just the complicated interplay of these specks of consciousness. It does not possess many of the attributes as yet; it is merely the beginning. For example, it has not become memory; but it is the sort of activity that makes the sort of records of which memory is born.

2

We cannot see far enough back to determine even approximately when these little combinations of consciousness, expressing the simplest sort of idea or direction or intention, become the individual,—where, as one might say, Me-ness begins.

It must be very far down indeed. Perhaps it is even at that first differentiation of all when the original two got direction in space and time. After all, sensation is merely comparison between one, however simple and small, and another. These little specks might each have grasped the fact of its Me-ness out of recognizing—through the mere fact of its reaction of force and motion—that there was another beside itself.

But this we can precicate confidently enough; that every speck added to a group introduces not only a new force into the combination, but also changes the interplay of the old ones. It does not matter how relatively small the newcomer is as compared to the mass it joins, it has its influence on making a new thing of it. This is as near a universal law as we can imagine. It obtains everywhere, both in small and in large. It is the fundamental of change and of progress. We can see it in gross by adding a spoonful of alcohol to a two hundred pound man: in small by introducing a single electron to an atom and changing gold into quicksilver. The interplay and interdependence of all forces in the universe are amazing.

Though we cannot, as we have said, see far enough to guess at the exact origin of the individual, we can at least make for ourselves a definition by which each may for himself decide the question. At some point, very far down in the scale, created things ceased being merely representatives or embodiments of the quality of consciousness which guarded their ideas, and became real entities. At some point self-ness began. The moment might be defined as that in which a thing begins to recognize itself as Me and not somebody or something else, and to fight with what facilities and weapons it may possess to remain Me. The microscopical ameba, from this point of view, is a Me; and he looks upon everything about him with reference to his Me. He notes whether it is hot or cold—according to him; wet or dry; and he tries to conduct himself with reference to those facts in the way best to conserve his Me-ness. As soon as he gets that far along, he has his job.

And that job is in essentials no different from your job and my job. It is simply to practice, with all the equipment he possesses, in being

Me. What more have we to do? We are all learning to steer by our own compass: to be completely Me.

CHAPTER 7

MANIFESTATIONS OF CONSCIOUSNESS

~

1

THE establishment of the separate individual in consciousness does not by any means, presuppose the enduring individual. We are hardly prepared to claim immortality[1] for every bee or ant or flower, for every frog or fish or ameba or rotifer that is born in its multiple billions every day in the year. The idea is logical enough; and if we were put to it off-hand we could not define why one created thing should have a soul and another not. But the extreme and ever growing multiplicity of individual entities does not fall within acceptable reason. As we go up in evolution numbers diminish. However convinced we may be as to human immortality, or however inclined some might be to ascribe an enduring quality to some of the animals, I doubt if many can be found who consider seriously the probability that the crowded forms of animated nature all represent lasting individualities. We are encouraged to look farther in an effort toward some definition that will satisfy this idea.

------

[1] We must for the purpose of discussion, and to avoid confusion, define immortality only as an individual continuance in the finite. The word "eternal" is at present as inunderstandable as infinite space. As to why we are justified in believing in survival in any case, see Chapter 9.

If, however, the individual is not always enduring, of what avail his sometimes desperate effort to survive, his marvels of ingenious adaptation to environment, his feeble but persistent gropings toward better correspondences with the world in which he finds himself? It would seem to be futile. Except through the very limited outlet of heredity and the still more limited opportunity of teaching and example, his personal efforts and acquirements would seem to be wasted, as far as any general scheme of things goes. How about it?

2

The difficulty is not so great when we go back to our earlier reasoning and consider what the individual really is. He is, at base, nothing less than a separate embodiment or manifestation of a certain quality of consciousness. He is always a portion of that quality; and must therefore retain a certain relationship to it. We have seen that consciousness, like life and substance, has gone through an evolution from simple to complex. That evolution has been brought about—as is all progress—by adaptation, trial and error, experience and memory. Through those, and all other developing factors, it has evolved its different qualities. How has consciousness done this? Through its individuals—its embodiments in sub-stance, its manifestations in life.

From this viewpoint we may well consider the individual as the awareness-mechanism of consciousness, but especially of the quality of consciousness which it manifests. Through it consciousness becomes aware of itself. It becomes cognizant of its Me-ness.

That is true of consciousness as a whole; it is also true of its qualities. Each projection into substance, in the form of an individual, is a mechanism by which consciousness becomes increasingly aware of itself. It is by use and experiment that things perfect themselves to the point of self-realization. That is a universal law. It is true of our own bodily functions. The ear is one of the awareness-mechanisms by which we realize certain aspects, not-ourselves, represented by sound. Some creatures have no perception of sound. Others have a very rudimentary apparatus. We ourselves are able only through slow development and education to distinguish between noise and music, between rudimentary melody and higher harmonies. Thus we become conscious of ever finer and finer differences or correspondences between the us and the not-us; and we do it by the development and refinement and education of our awareness-mechanism.

Considering individual manifestations of consciousness as, first, expressions of the qualities consciousness has developed; and second, awareness-mechanisms of consciousness, our difficulties are more or less resolved. Consciousness develops new qualities which express themselves in new forms. The new forms are, so to speak, new or more fully refined senses by which consciousness becomes self-aware. It is a reciprocating process.

The function of the ephemeral individual, then, is also two-fold, It embodies forth its own quality of consciousness. Whatever that quality is, whatever it comprises, whatever it has developed or acquired, whatever wisdom it possesses is the creature's birthright. But also the latter functions in its environment; adapts itself; perhaps does something on its own account quite original with itself; something not inherited. As it is itself an awareness-mechanism, consciousness on the side of its quality must profit by that achievement. Its excursion into originality, its experience—successful or unsuccessful—with new conditions, become part of the knowledge and possession of its quality of consciousness. If it has stumbled upon or acquired or devised something of real value, it seems quite possible that the acquisition might be included in the equipment of its successors.

This equipment, which represents self-awareness on the side of any particular quality of consciousness, we call instinct. The individual comes into existence endowed with a complicated knowledge of just how to go about things. In some of the higher animals such knowledge is assisted by teaching of parents and by imitation, but it can be observed in all its purity in the insect world. In his observations on the sand wasp Fabre gives us a good example.

The larva of this insect needs a living but immobile host in which to develop. To provide such a thing the parent must sting its prey just enough to paralyze it, but not enough to kill it. If the sand wasp possessed no instinct in the matter but must act entirely from reason, he would first have to go through an extraordinary education. He would have to take a course in the anatomy of the caterpillar. The caterpillar is sometimes formidably armed and stronger than its attacker. There are only a few nerve centers where a sting brings the desired result. After having learned where these nerve centers are, and how they can best be got at, our student would have to take another course in the action of poison. Too big a dose will kill, too small a dose will not have the desired effect. Furthermore, the different nerve centers require differing doses. In one place one stab of the sting is right; in another it takes two; in still another several more. Nevertheless, the sand wasp emerges from its cocoon and goes about its highly skilled business unerringly. Its parents who might have taught it have long been dead: its solitary habit precludes its learning so delicate a business by repeated example; it has little chance for practice, for ordinarily it must succeed at its first attempt or be in grave danger.

This is a simple, though striking, instance. The life business of bees is another; the polity of an ant colony still another; the reaching of a newborn child for its mother's breast quite as good a third. The world is crowded with them. Most natural history is observation of the action of this type of intelligence.

Nevertheless, though this endowment of instinct comes complete to each creature, the knowledge it represents has been slowly acquired and developed. It is, we say, innate in that creature; born with it. That is true. But it is born with it because its quality of consciousness has acquired the wisdom as part of itself; and therefore anything that really embodies that quality must possess its wisdom.

Furthermore, this wisdom has been bought as any wisdom is bought. No sand wasp, even though endowed with full reasoning powers, could possibly work out its complicated technique.

There are too many chances for mistake, and mistakes are dangerous. In his first uninformed struggle with the caterpillar his random stinging would have one chance in a thousand of hitting the right spot, and one in many thousands more of delivering just the correct amount of poison. But if we can conceive of the possibility of correlating the experience of a million sand wasps, we might be able to get at something through a process of elimination. And then try it again with a million more. Nature is prodigal of her creatures. Why note She is learning.

This hypothesis, of course, implies that instincts are themselves subject to development. For a long time the contrary was held to be the case. It was acknowledged that the civil administration of bee colonies or ant colonies was very perfect, but it was assumed that it was fixed and never changed. Now later investigation has showed us that our conclusions have been drawn too hastily. We have observed over too brief a period as compared to the life history of the race. Insects do invent, do adapt, do better their methods when confronted with more favorable or radically better conditions. Perez, Marchel, and Peckham[21] have shown this very conclusively in the case of many insects, but

---

[2] Works to be found in any good library.

especially of the bee. That creature, whose system of cooperative industry and government has long been considered to be a brilliant example of the completely adapted and standardized, is shown not only to have developed and radically improved his methods within our own knowledge of his history, but to be capable of the most ingenious adaptations or inventions when offered fresh opportunity.

CHAPTER 8

TRIAL AND ERROR

~

1

WE have, as we hinted in the previous chapter, no reason in logic so far for making any distinction between individuals as respects immortality. There seems—as far as we have conducted our argument—to be no right we can arrogate to ourselves that will justify us in drawing a line and claiming that all creatures one side the line have souls, and all on the other side of the line have not. Nevertheless, we recoil against carrying the logic out to its uttermost. It is more a matter of common-sense than of pride of position. I personally would have no objection to every ant on the hillside possessing an immortal soul, and I should be ready to admit the thing as possible; but I shall not be inclined to believe it. Common-sense is far from being always an infallible guide, but it is a pretty good indicator to stop, look and listen. Whatever it has to say is at least worth examination.

Since we have, up to now, no logical reason to deny any individual immortality, provided we admit that any individual whatever is immortal;[1] but since common-sense interposes a doubt, we must examine the whole question to see if there is any specific thing, clearly distinguishing, which we can ascribe to those creatures we think to be immortal, and which we will find to be absent in all others. In advance

---

[1] See Chapter 9 for the reasons why we should predicate continuity at all.

we must anticipate, from our studies in other directions, that even if we find such an element it will be exceedingly improbable that it will furnish us with a rule by which to draw our definite line. In all nature we find, not hard and fast divisions, but gradual shadings off. We cannot say where the vegetable kingdom ends and the animal kingdom begins; we cannot say where instinct is replaced or supplemented by reason; we cannot draw a hard and fast line anywhere. But perhaps we can get. a basis of definition.

2

The two elements that develop and make effective consciousness of any sort are experience and memory. Experience is the being acted upon by things or the attempting of things either successfully or unsuccessfully. But experience is not much good unless one remembers it; for only thus can one correlate and compare and utilize and incorporate into growth. It is also true that for continuous consciousness memory is necessary. Indeed we may say that consciousness is continuous only as long as and to the extent that it remembers. That it may be intermittent without being discontinuous, in the sense we now mean, is of course obvious. We do not seem to remember anything when we are asleep: but we do carry on a continuous consciousness by means of memory. This very broad consideration may be said to cover the entire question of continuity; whether of a brief flash of earth life as exhibited in the ephemeride, or in the continuity raised to the nth power which we call immortality.

Here, perhaps, is something to go on. All growth comes through experience utilized by memory. That obtains in the slow and groping progress, extended through the thousands of years, which led from the ocean's slime to the first ameba, as well as in the faster evolution of the human race from ox cart to airplane. The two are equally important parts of a reciprocating mechanism. In the human being, where we can best observe them, they appear to us as almost completely exhibited in the individual mechanism of each person.

But when we descend far enough in the scale to have reached those creatures whose activities seem to be nearly or quite all instinct, we find what may be interpreted as a division of labor between the creature and the quality of consciousness which it embodies. The creature experiences; the quality of consciousness remembers. Whatever the creature experiences the quality is cognizant of, for the simple reason that the creature is—as we have seen—the quality's awareness-mechanism. Whatever the quality is cognizant of, is henceforth part of its self-awareness, part of itself. And as its creatures are embodiments or manifestations of itself, they must subsequently acquire, as birthright, whatever the quality has gained. In its capacity as guardian of the Idea, the quality remembers—must remember in the sense that memory is a storehouse of utilizable experience.

We have seen before how the quality remembers. It has compressed within the single germ cell all the experiences of the human race in its long course of evolution, so, that one by one, in orderly progression, they are brought forth and passed by or utilized. It has even remembered some of the mistakes, or near-mistakes or expedients, so that we find them completely or partially embodied in what we call vestigial remains. It has remembered faithfully all the chance encounters and experiments and failures and rare, occasional, blundering successes of the sand wasp, and has passed on the results of that memory in the form of an exquisitely perfect technique. No individual human being has any recollection of those experiences, no individual sand wasp. Man does not recall even his own brief reptilian phase when he possessed a three chambered heart, or his equally brief piscatorial phase when he boasted gill clefts. The sand wasp has no records of the millions of times he essayed and perished. Nevertheless, in the quality of consciousness, of which these two creatures are expressions, all the memories of past experience on the part of individuals have been retained and are now used.

Indeed, in the very lowest forms of life it is legitimate to doubt whether the individual remembers much even of its own experience. We do not remember a very large proportion of ours. The creature functions. In that functioning it experiences things that happen, and acts as an awareness-mechanism for the very simple quality of consciousness which it expresses. The storage of impressions, as one might call it, is in the quality, not in the individual. The only reason we have for believing that the impressions are stored anywhere at all is because the Idea of that creature seems to expand and modify in accordance with the experience of the millions of specimens of his kind. He proceeds in evolution. The later examples of the Idea are an improvement on the first examples. And the improvement is in accordance with the experience of the first examples. Those experiences are not taught; they are not imitated; they are not embodied in the first instance of heredity. The Idea is modified.

We are now at last prepared to define instinct. It is a sort of racial wisdom, evolved from the memory of the experience brought to any quality of consciousness by its innumerable creatures.

Again we can find our perfect example in the sand wasp. An individual wasp, or a thousand of them, or a million, meet with utter disaster in ignorant attempts to fulfil—or better fulfil—the requirements of their being. They proceed by trial and error—mostly fatal error—in their search for a host that shall be both living and immobile. At great cost of life they attempt a multitude of impossible experiments. Each of these fatal accidents is an experience, unavailing to the individual that thus perishes, but each adding through quality memory to the sum of knowledge of what *cannot* be done. And that knowledge is part of the equipment of the wasp quality's succeeding manifestations; so that henceforward wasps by *instinct* do not try that particular thing again. Thus by almost infinitesimal steps—and through the contribution of innumerable lives—the true and only possible method is approached; until at last we see in the perfection we have admired that sure and accurate lethal stab on the one possible spot that shall assure the beautiful completeness of the wasp's life cycle. All from experience: all from memory.

Progress.

3

That progress is in several directions. It is toward the perfection of each quality of consciousness: it is toward the ever more accurate expression in substance of the idea which that quality of consciousness contains: it is toward the complete evocation of all potentialities in that quality of consciousness. In other words, consciousness perfects that particular idea; it perfects the embodiment of the idea; it works out all the possibilities of the idea. It does this by experience and memory. The individual creatures which embody it are its mechanisms of awareness. We might say that any quality of consciousness is, in essence, striving toward complete self-awareness. It seeks to fill out its own level. That is its own especial job, the thing that is most important.

That is why,—at least in the lower and simpler and more specialized forms of life,—the species is so much more important than the specimen. That is why nature is so lavish; why she is content to spend a million small lives that a single one may survive.

Why not? These lower forms touch individual existence as dust motes touch individual existence—as far as our attention goes—when they eddy in and out of a sun ray. They flash for a greater or lesser period; and are obscured. They have gained nothing as motes during their brief life of illumination; they have lost nothing as motes when they slip out into the shadow. But they have added, perhaps, some little bit of beauty in the eye of the beholder; and so their very evanescence has fulfilled a purpose. In a similar fashion the billions of ants and bees and all the buzzing and humming and swarming and teeming life that crowds everywhere slips into and out of individual existence, adding to the memory of their quality of consciousness, enlarging their own Intention, so to speak, by the tiny bit of experience they gain as individuals. And also, in the Pattern, contributing to the experience and memory of those things and beings with which their little circumscribed individual lives may bring them in contact. Why should not nature be lavish of life? It fulfils.

4

By following this thought just a little farther we get a glimpse of one of the processes by which evolution may proceed.

Conceive that some quality of consciousness, through its awareness-mechanisms, proceeding on through the ages, does develop its potentialities to a near-perfection. It is so rich in its store of experience and memory and the wisdom appropriate to it that, as to that particular idea, consciousness is almost completely self-aware. It is exuberant with the beauty of its own completeness.

But this very completeness, like any exuberance, is suggestive, so to speak. Dimly, outside its own central Idea, other ideas are faintly hinted. Consciousness seeks another mechanism to embody these new ideas, through which to become more fully self-aware as to them. Modifications appear. Or, when the idea is a fresh one, with radical enough departures from what has been, we have a brand new species.

Thus another quality of consciousness is born. And this quality, like all new things, is at first a trifle hazy as to itself and its ideas. It must develop toward perfection,—again through its manifestations, its awareness-mechanisms. From it, likewise, must come those brief flashes into material individuality—each bringing its little gift of function fulfilled. It, too, must fill out its level to the point of exuberance. And so on up.

Evolution.

CREDO

This conception of the development in evolution going on in the qualities of consciousness, the molding dynamism, the thing that is compressed in the germ cell that antecedes the human embryo, the idea that formed the butterfly out of the liquefied raw material to which the caterpillar was reduced, will,—if accepted,—explain many discrepancies. We need no longer search for or ascribe importance to "missing links." We need no longer puzzle over mutations. We need no longer be surprised at the sudden emergence of new faculties or powers; nor need we wonder at the spectacle of animated life abruptly leaving the sea or taking to the air. The orderly progression of evolution has gone on, but its sequences must be sought in a developing self-awareness of consciousness. The things we see and study are merely such expressions of the Idea as have been necessary for the process to go on.

CHAPTER 9

THE QUESTION OF SURVIVAL

~

1

BEFORE going on we must examine to see if we are justified in a belief in continuity after death. That belief has always been held by the vast majority of mankind. It has been questioned at times, it is being questioned, but in the long run it has held its own. Man expects to survive his bodily decease. Is that expectation justified? Is it a deep and true instinct born into him from the knowledge and wisdom and memory of his human quality? Or is it the mere expression of a hope, based on an ineradicable egocentricity?

Many attempts have been made, in many directions, to gain some assurance on this important point. Though the field of psychic research has covered much that has to do with merely an extension of man's own powers, or with an explanation of the heretofore mysterious; nevertheless its chief effort has undoubtedly been toward definite proof of the survival of personality. Material science,—generally with negative results,—has devoted much attention to the same thing. Pure philosophy has argued in endless volumes. A few have thus become convinced that they possess indisputable proof. Nevertheless, in the long run and to the majority of people, belief in continuity is an article of faith rather than of proof. It is accepted on authority, it is accepted on instinct, it is a matter of belief held wholeheartedly or hopefully or doubtfully or provisionally or fearfully, as the case may be.

Personally I should be willing to let it rest at that. I myself have that deep inner conviction of survival beyond this earth life, and I trust that conviction. As far as my own attitude toward the universe is concerned, and all it implies, I am quite ready to proceed on that basis.

However it does not seem to me necessary to proceed on that basis. The biggest things in existence we have always to take for a time on faith, adopting them in the nature of provisional hypotheses as working premises, accepting the inner conviction, as we accept hunger and thirst, as true guides to our necessities, but this I do firmly believe: that nothing finite is ultimately inunderstandable. All occult things are capable of de-occultization. The whole progress of human knowledge is such a process. What the middle ages looked upon as miracles, we use as everyday commonplaces of applied science. What we today consider as vague mysteries will undoubtedly in their turn, when the time comes, take their places in the everyday body of knowledge. In the long last, faith is always overtaken by understanding.

2

Perhaps in time psychic research will furnish us all with the indubitable proof it seeks. I am inclined to think it will. It is a young science. In the meantime it seems to me that a very definite step may be taken in our intellectual estimate of the situation. Let us examine the whole question of personal survival beyond death in order to determine, if we may, whether any general and indubitable principles from our store of knowledge may not apply.

The disbeliever in continuity after death,—or the one who has not in full the inner conviction of survival,—considers that the personal consciousness that now animates him suffers at death an extinction, an obliteration, a dissolution similar to the dissolution that overtakes the physical body. The animating principle passes back into the source from which it came; the consciousness which has been his rejoins whatever stuff of which it is made; the physical body disintegrates and becomes again an indistinguishable part of the physical substance of which the world is composed. He cannot, in the light of his own physics, predicate a dissolution of these elements into nothingness, however. If he is rational in his thinking, he must admit the law of the conservation of matter and energy. These things may change form completely, but they must remain as part of the sum total of things. The physical constituents of his body, could they be carefully segregated and preserved, would weigh the same; the force with which he was animated, could it be saved and measured, would measure the same. Nothing is lost: it is a remergence into that from which he was made. He believes that all this takes place at the moment of his physical death.

Except as to the single last point we can agree with him in general. Continuity as an individual separate from all other individuals "forever," in the infinite sense, is as inconceivable as infinity itself. Infinity must be a unity. We cannot conceive of space bounded by a wall; there must be something beyond the wall. We cannot conceive of space going on forever without a limit. Similarly we cannot conceive time ever ending;—or never ending! We cannot comprehend this; and we should not try. But this at least we can apprehend, that infinity whether of space or time or consciousness or whatever of reality, must be one thing, comprehending in itself all that may be. Otherwise it at once ceases to be infinity. If there is but one separate thing, and all else, then we have the finite. Therefore we cannot avoid the thought, no matter how little we may comprehend it, that in the infinite at least there must be remergence of all separateness; I must repeat, we cannot comprehend this, but we can apprehend it.

Therefore with the materialist's conception on this score the believer in continuity diverges in only one respect. The former would place his point of remergence at the moment of physical dissolution. He would say that that point makes the merging and coincidence of the individual consciousness or life or spirit with the All consciousness, the Infinite, the Absolute. He limits his conception of continuity to the thing he can at present see. The other, on the contrary, continues his individual into a future which the physical eye cannot behold. Whether that continuance extends but a fleeting moment beyond its dissociation with the physical, or out into unguessed aeons of time has little to do with the matter in essential. For, as we have seen, in the strict sense of the term no bit of separateness can endure "forever," in the literal sense, except as by successive and expanding growth and inclusion it tends in the infinite to become itself the All-conscious.

Thus, I think, all must have at least a common starting point from which to move forward.

3

We can also with all confidence predicate another apprehension, rather than comprehension, of what lies outside our limit markers of time and space. We cannot avoid the conception that for some inscrutable purpose, which we are incompetent to understand, the Infinite has by time and space conditioned itself, at least in one phase; and that within those conditions it has developed, and is continuing to develop, increasing self-awareness through the individual manifestations of an ever-growing Idea. Starting, in space and time, always with the extremest simplicity, it runs through an orderly evolution to great complexity. Matter, beginning with proton and electron, gradually builds up into the (presumably) ninety-two elements, which in turn combine in varying proportions and conditions into a bewildering variety of substances. Life proceeds from its first faint stirrings of what seems to us one kind of force, through a swarm of embodiments, to its multiform manifestations as we know it. Consciousness too progresses in evolution from the dull mechanical reaction to natural law up to the flexible and startling embodiment we know in the human being. All things we are capable of observing, whether by our physical senses or in the inner processes of mind and feeling, seem to be subject to this same law. Beginning with the simplest conceivable elements they proceed by expansion, by development and by accretion, to carry out a definite and orderly evolution.

And, furthermore, we perceive that this evolution is indeed orderly. There are no shortcuts. In the case of those smaller processes which we can view as a whole, and as completed, we find the return to the starting point with enrichment of experience, with function fulfilled, is always around the arc of a circle. This point has been touched on in an earlier chapter. We must traverse the whole circumference before we find ourselves back again at the original simplicity. This again is true in all cosmos, whether we view it from the standpoint of matter, of life or of consciousness. It obtains in physical nature, it obtains in our own psychological experiences, it obtains in our laboratory experiments, it obtains in the lives of men and the lives of planets. The completed circle is more than a symbol; it is a universal fact. In the case of any creature, any law, any idea, anything palpable or impalpable that *develops*, this rise into complexity and return enriched to simplicity holds good.

Nor, to repeat, can one cut across in a return to the starting point. He merely brings back his complexities with him. The scientist still in the intricacies of experiment cannot state his problem simply: only when it has ceased to be a problem, only after he has completed his experiments, can he express his thesis with the simple lucidity of one who knows. If it be acknowledged that radioactivity may by the subtraction of electrons result in an elemental resimplification, the process cannot be otherwise than orderly. Uranium, by any conceivable process, could not at once throw off ninety-one of its free electrons to become hydrogen. In its loss of constituents it must pass back down the arc,—ninety-one UX2, ninety for thorium and so on. It is an invariable process that may be studied anywhere in nature, anywhere in activity of any sort whether social, material, historical, psychological, biological,—what you will. One has only to look about one.

4

That is the second consideration we are to notice. The third follows naturally from it, and is as susceptible to observation in whatever direction one looks, and whatever the type of process one examines. It is this:

No creature, no law, no idea, no thing palpable or impalpable can abruptly, at any point short of the completed circle, break off to return to its inception or origin. In other words, again, there are no shortcuts.

The circle of function may, of course, be large or small. It may, as we have seen, be a complicated building one by one of near a hundred physical elements from the primordial ether, their perfection through embodiment, and their gradual and graceful resimplification through radioactivity: the whole process consuming aeons of time and extending in prospect beyond the vision of all but the farthest speculation. Or its circumscribing may be performed almost in the space of a breath. All the processes of nature seem to be laid before us for our edification on this point. We can see the process in any size that suits us, in any magnitude fitted for our examination. But always it is the completed circle. So universal is this law in the cases of all things we are capable of understanding that we have no intellectual right, short of an absolute proof to the contrary, to deny its application to those things we do not comprehend.

And from these considerations we can deduce that differentiations of consciousness also must have a circle of function to round out, that they cannot return to original simplicity—and hence to original source—until their functions are fulfilled. No such differentiation in the finite can remerge into the All-consciousness of the infinite until that particular circle of evolution,—*of which we are part*—has been closed. At no point short of a completion of the whole scheme can any one of those differentiations break down and merge with the Absolute. They are, and must remain, intact.

5

This may be conceived to be true of differentiations of consciousness, what we have called qualities of consciousness. But that by no means logically follows as to the particular manifestations of each quality. It may be true of the bee quality, in essence, but not necessarily of the individual bees. The Idea is intact and must follow in its circle the rest of finity, but the individual may quite satisfactorily and completely round its own little circle of function and remerge, at the point of regained simplicity, with its quality. It will continue as an individual as long as— *and only as long as*—its own circle is incomplete.

The duration of continuity, then, in the case of the individual, may be considered as coincidental with the complete rounding of its own circle, the complete fulfilling of its individual function, whatever it may be.

6

The question of survival thus at once defines itself. It must become evident that whether any one thing completes its circle within the circumstances with which we are familiar, and before our physical eyes; or whether those eyes are seeing only a segment which rounds its completeness beyond our vision, depends entirely on whether or not we are observing a function completely fulfilled.

CHAPTER 10

INDIVIDUALITY AND CONTINUITY

~

1

IN the case of the lower forms of life we do observe the function
fulfilled. It is obviously simple and physical. Its contribution as an
awareness-mechanism to consciousness is completely made in its
life struggle. From examination of its structure, its habits, its equipment
we are able to evaluate all its possibilities. We can find in it no faculty
nor aptitude which has not its full correspondence in the present
physical environment. In no individual of the species can we discover
any special and unique talent or genius which its personal extinction
will remove from the field of effort. It is completely interchangeable with
any other individual of its kind. Any robin will do at the place where
the robin effort is needed. Remove one fish and substitute another—any
other of that species—and the complete fish business will go forward.
Since this is so, there can appear to exist no reason why the individual
separateness should display any further continuity beyond the obvious
purpose that has brought it into being. The quality of consciousness
which it embodies has not fulfilled its function, and therefore goes on;
but it can do so quite as well through other individuals,—any other
individuals.

It is only when the separate individual of a species develops an
originality special and unique to itself; when it is no longer a completely
interchangeable part with the other manifestations of its Idea; when

79

it obviously possesses qualities or attributes or powers or obligations of development which sweep the arc of its circle beyond the highest common denominator of its kind, that we are entitled even to surmise any continuity beyond what we can see.

As to what this may actually mean we shall examine in the next chapter. For the moment let us take it as it stands, and see where it leads.

Let us conceive an individual creature, then, of some species that has by its own effort added something of possibility to the sum total of the normal possibilities of its species. It has thereby enlarged its own fulfilment beyond the normal and ordinary fulfilment of its kind. This fulfilment must be rounded out. If it has added a single aptitude or attribute or even potentiality, that potentiality must be worked out before its owner can be remerged. The circle must be completed before that creature can have followed the law of all cosmos,—started from primal simplicity, developed all its complexities, and so enriched by function fulfilled returned to its primal simplicity. And this, as we have seen, is in all things prerequisite to remergence with source.

2

In the lower creatures,—what we have called the interchangeable creatures,—the complete rounding out of all potentialities before this remergence with source seems to be coincidental with physical life. The circle of fulfilment and the circle of life seem accurately to superimpose one on the other. Furthermore, the normal span of physical life seems to be only just adequate for this complete rounding out. Each adapts itself neatly to the other's dimension. This may be most clearly observed in the simplest cases of the very lowest forms of life; but once the principle is grasped one can trace its action in higher and higher species. That is to say, one can trace it up to the point where the individual specimens of the species are not completely standardized: where in every case one specimen could not be substituted for any other specimen without alteration of the scheme.

Since, then, the fulfilled functioning of those powers, or attributes, or abilities or possibilities which belong to the species as a whole do so accurately fill just to the brim the duration of physical life, it must follow that any added powers or attributes or possibilities in the case of one Or more super-specimens of that species must require more room for completed functioning than the ordinary standardized specimens require. In other words, in these particular cases the circumference is enlarged, the cycle extended. It can no longer accurately superimpose on the physical circle. The duration of that particular creature's fulfilment must extend at least a little beyond the physical life we see. It may not be for long: the arc may extend but a slender new moon into the invisible; but it is a definite continuity for all that. Before that bit of separate consciousness can have returned to its starting point, which it must do before it can remerge with its source, it must have finished its effort begun.

As long as we confine our consideration to the very lowest forms of life capable of this individual development we are compelled to admit the possibility that completed functioning of these new and feeble but individual attributes might take place, not in an extension of continuity beyond death, but in a more active life this side of death. But as we raise our vision up the scale, we begin to see that, no matter how we may crowd our hours, the circle of physical existence is becoming too contracted to admit complete fulfilment. No matter how active and varied an existence the creature may live, it literally cannot find room to fulfil not only its specific functions, which it has in common with all its kind, but also its acquired individual functions. It needs; it must have more space. The segment of its circle must push into the invisible.

3

This is not immortality, as we loosely define it, but it is a continuity beyond what we can see. It is what we might call a germ of immortality.[1]

Furthermore, this is to be noted: that the segment of the circle which does so extend into the invisible is just that portion which is individual. It is what has been added by the creature's own and unique effort. And so we come upon a great and illuminating thought: that any continuity beyond the physical life is not an inherent gift, but an earned thing. It is gained by the individual and personal effort of each creature, *and in no other way!* Whatever life there may be beyond death is the direct result of individual and personal construction, by effort of free will; applied, perhaps through a long evolution, but nevertheless a matter entirely of individual building.

---

[1] See Chapter 11 for further discussion of this point.

4

In the higher forms of consciousness, as we know them, then, there would seem to be two circles of fulfilment. One belongs to the quality of consciousness, the species. The individual holds it in common with all other creatures of his kind. If he held nothing else, he would remerge, cease to exist, when that circle is rounded out, which would be at the moment of physical death.

The other circle is peculiar and individual to himself, and is the result of his own effort. Its diameter is a precise measure of that effort. The continuity it represents may be much or it may be little; but it is a definite achievement. The thing he has builded has enlarged his circle so that its necessary rounding out will extend his duration definitely and personally and individually.

Nevertheless, that circle also must at any given moment have a defined radius. There must be a point in time when it will have completed itself. A sufficient knowledge and intelligence should theoretically be able to predict any creature's "expectation of life" as the life insurance people have it, at any one time. Such a forecast would, however, be accurate only for that one time. It seems likely that in any duration so gained there must be so many opportunities for further effort and further building that a continuous process of enlargement must take place. Except in the hypothetical case of a creature that absolutely and completely "stood pat" on past achievement; except one ceased all effort, relapsed into a dead inertia, contenting oneself with a stolid concentration within one's present self, there must be a gradual and certain extension of the expectation of life.

For whatever expectation of life has been achieved by effort must be fulfilled. The circle, such as it now is, must be rounded out. Nothing that has been earned of immortality can be destroyed or lost. Even if one sat tight and lived out only the possibilities, he at present possesses, he must fulfil those possibilities completely. Though it is theoretically possible for the soul to be extinguished as a separate and individual entity, it is only possible at the end of its expectation of immortality based upon its past building. And even then, only in the almost impossible event that it become inert, deadened to its opportunities and obligations of increasing life.

From that point of view the so-called deterrent or destructive or retrogressive influences and activities and omissions, which broadly we call evil, are not really disintegrating forces. They can have no effect on whatever meed of continuity the soul has actually gained. But they may be very definitely preventives of immortality's extension.

5

In that thought may be found a tremendous inspiration. We have no birthright of life; but we have a definite opportunity. As no two creatures of the higher orders are precisely alike, so the immediate expectation of continuity of no two creatures can be exactly the same. Some have already sketched wider circles than others. Even in the human quality of consciousness people differ widely in their states of development. Some are what one might call young souls; others are what one might call old souls.[2] The young souls, whatever their strength and vigor, and whatever their possibilities of extension through the exercise of those attributes, must have descried, at this moment, a smaller circle than those of higher development. If the whole process could be stopped short right now, and the Scheme go forward solely by the momentum already acquired, the undeveloped would continue a much shorter period than the developed who have long builded. But the whole process is not stopped short: it is going on. There seems to me every reason to believe that any human being, except possibly in the rarest of instances, is sufficiently endowed with a surplus of vitality over the demands on it, with enough of capacity to receive and of energy to accomplish to be able to enlarge his consciousness ahead of his own proper timepiece, so to speak.

His circle enlarges in advance of his overtaking it.

Barring conscious and persistent contrary effort on his part, he seems probably destined to extend his continuity until his own circle is coincident with the circle of the finite itself.

He has, in general, a decent margin to work on. Already even the lowest type of human being has come into possession of faculties and tendencies and attributes the fulfilling of which is manifestly impossible in the physical life. The segment of his arc sweeps widely into the invisible. It would be difficult to find a man so mean that one could not say of him that if physical death really ended him, he was not cut off untimely. And we would say it because of the profound realization that seemingly a broad preparation has been made for which there is no room for conclusion.

---

[2] See Chapter 12 for a discussion of reincarnation.

CHAPTER 11

MEMORY AND ATTRIBUTES

~

1

NOW let us take up the whole question from a quite different standpoint. Let us go back to the individual. By the criterion we have as yet imperfectly outlined, at what point in the scale—if at all—does it persist as an individual beyond the brief manifestation in substance which we observe?

Duration would go on as long as the individual could remember itself. That is well enough as a definition, or a handle to take hold of, but it does not get us far in our answer. As nearly as we can reason it seems probable—at least rational—that the very lowest forms of life are, as individuals, merely awareness-mechanisms of their quality. They are projections in substance of that particular intention, as far as it has developed up to that point. Their lives are conducted by a series of reactions to stimuli. Those reactions are in accordance with the wisdom of their race, rather than with any personal judgments of their own. Their consciousness is the consciousness possessed by their quality. They are like feelers sent out experimentally into substance. They have *individual life,* in that they are separate things possessed of a sense of separateness; but they probably have not as yet *personal* life, in the sense of exercising intelligent choice through memory. Their appearance of choice is most likely conditioned by the stimuli they receive; and that there is a choice at all is due to race experience and wisdom—through their quality of consciousness—as to which particular reaction to which particular stimulus is most advantageous. There have been many interesting experiments on these lines, notably as to the invariable reactions of aquarium fish to lights. So striking were the results that one of our best known naturalists was carried away by them to the point of absurdity, and gravely postulated that the singing of birds indicated nothing of individual joy and rapture, but was merely a mechanical and automatic response to such things as the rays of the sun or a warm current of air!

That, by any sober examination, seems nonsense. Things do not work along quite such direct lines when we consider so complex a creature as the bird. But in the case of the simplest organisms we know, there seems no reason to ascribe anything like memory.[1] There is no occasion for memory. The ameba does not need to remember what to do the next time a drought threatens or it turns cold. He knew what to do the first time, quite perfectly. His conduct in the exigencies of life is carefully arranged for him by his reactions; and they in turn are provided for by his physical and nervous equipment; and they, once more, are the epitome of the wisdom possessed by his rather limited quality of consciousness. There is, to repeat, no necessity of his having a memory. He is an *individual*, in that at any given moment he realizes and acts upon his separateness from the things about him. It is to be doubted that he is *a person* in the sense of remembering himself even from moment to moment.

That obtains to our apparent satisfaction only very low down in the scale. As far as I have been able to discover no experiments devised up to now have shown the slightest trace of memory in such creatures. But we do not have to climb very far before we begin to find such traces. Miss Gertrude White by means of colored discs showed distinct evidences of memory in minnows. She suspended food before a red disc and imitation food before a blue disc. After a number of experiences the minnows learned to come whenever a red disc was offered, but ignored

---

[1] Nevertheless, certain experiments render this point not at all certain. It may be that certain protozoa exhibit learning-process through memory. The point is unimportant to the general reasoning.

It merely pushes the exact point lower down. Therefore I retain the above illustration. See Jennings, Behavior of the Lower Organisms; and Ladd and Woodsworth, Elements of Physiological Psychology.

the blue. Professor Yerkes experimented along similar lines with a turtle "of retiring disposition." On the path of its habitual retreat toward its rest he planted a simple maze. The turtle's first penetration of this maze was of course by blundering chance, and took 35 minutes. On its next attempt, two hours later, however, it got through in 15 minutes. The third trial, also after a two hours intermission, consumed 5 minutes. By the twentieth experiment the turtle knew its route and made the journey in 45 seconds. This was of course true experience and memory wisdom.

To be sure the fish and the turtle are comparatively high in the scale, but the examples are good ones. Similar experiments on much lower forms of life would undoubtedly enable us more closely to approximate the line—or rather the broad and indeterminate band—where the individual becomes the person, where the purely reflex manifestation of the quality of consciousness requires the rudiments of a memory. It would be found wherever the creature needs a memory.

2

We must next pause to notice for a moment a simple and obvious idea. We have become accustomed to the various qualities into which consciousness itself has developed, which qualities represent themselves or manifest themselves in the various kinds of creatures and things in the finite universe. It is now necessary to note that each of these qualities of consciousness itself possesses certain *attributes.*

That is self-evident. The dog quality possesses the attribute of loyalty, of affinity for human beings, of pugnacity, of passion for investigation, and what-not, the sum of all of which make up his essential dogginess. He also develops in the course of his life experience many other attributes which though present as potentialities at the beginning were entirely latent. The human quality possesses a myriad of attributes, some of which have been developed to a very high point, others of which are in the course of development, and still others of which are merely shadowed as possibilities. But either as a dog, or as a human being, or as anything else in creation, each is composed of the sum of all the attributes of its quality of consciousness. They are *all* there, whether developed or not, in every physical manifestation. If, for convenience, we consider the dog quality to consist of X number of attributes, then in order to have an expression of that quality in matter—in order to have any puppies—it is necessary that the whole number be present. If one

87

could build a puppy as one builds a Ford car, one could not assemble the puppy with X—I attributes. If we are to consider the puppy as the manifestation in substance of the dog quality, then obviously there could be no such manifestation unless the dog quality is completely represented. Otherwise it would not be the dog quality. When we went to work to assemble that puppy, we would have to rummage around in the dog quality to find him a full set of parts.

Any quality of consciousness is the sum of all its attributes: all these attributes must be present potentially in every created thing representing that quality.

3

Now let us go back to the first individual—whatever we may assume it to be—that shows even a trace of personal memory. By analogy with all other methods of development we are safe in assuming that it will not be much of a memory and that it will not endure very long. Perhaps from one moment to the next would be its scope. Little by little, as the creature expands its new faculty by use, it will reciprocally find more use for it. That new use will in turn extend it. The creature remembers to-night what happened to it in the morning, and adapts itself to the situation as well as it can, not solely by the mechanical reflex of its instinct, but also by its memory of a situation. For the first time the tremendously stimulating power of individual intelligence comes into play. And the individual, to as yet a very limited extent, has become a person.

As I conceive it, this extension of memory would be very slow. It is probable that a long evolution must take place before the creature can remember back very far. He would be quite well along in the scale before his duration of personality would extend from one end of his life to the other, before he could remember the course of his days here on earth.

But long before that would happen he would have gained the great privilege of being able through his own intelligent effort to enrich his contribution to his quality of consciousness. As an individual person, not as a mere feeler or antenna projected by the quality into substance, not as a mechanical awareness-mechanism only, he is able to construct experience. That is his own gift, according to his own energy and capacity. It represents the germ of many things,—the power of choice that will in time dignify itself as free will; personality; immortality itself.

Note: I say the germ of these things; not necessarily the things themselves. If all the signposts of nature point in the right direction these too must be incubated and guarded and fostered and developed before they are born as actual things.

In order that an individual creature be in itself a permanently enduring creature, it must possess *in enduring form*[2] all the attributes of its quality. It would not be sufficient to possess even X—I of these attributes. If the I lacks, the machine could not be assembled as a completely enduring machine. Even if we conceive that some individual creature, because of great strength of personality, died carrying with it back to its quality of consciousness some enduring attribute individual to itself, we could not consider that creature as a whole to be immortal unless it was complete in itself. It might have contributed into its quality in enduring form one or more of the "makings" of a new manifestation, so to speak, but not all of the makings. We may conceive, however, that at some point in the general upward progress of qualities of consciousness there comes a time when the individual leaving life and merging back into its quality, as the dust mote left the sun, carries with it a little self-contained glow of its own, so to speak. This glow is very faint and very simple. It is a resultant of specialized experience which wears grooves deep enough to contain a little memory in one form or another that is peculiar to itself. Perhaps it may also result from especial effort of some sort. At any rate, that particular mote, drifting out of the sun ray, is not completely blotted out by the darkness. But that which persists beyond the specialized earth life is not a complete individual manifestation of its quality. It does not contain in itself as an entity all the X attributes. It is woefully incomplete, a mere fragment, a specific emphasizing of what by chance or effort or exuberance of life has been especially developed. If, to resume our figure, we were to assemble a new creature of this species from all the attributes of that particular quality, we would be able to use these ready-made enduring parts in our construction, and they would be the same parts that had been used before; but we would have to make other parts to complete the machine. *Or perhaps we might find other ready-made parts from some other scrapped machine, and use them.* These few things that may, through a vitality gained by development, be conceived to have survived individually the physical dissolution of the entity are not themselves an Individual. But, persisting, they may become the nucleus for another

---

[2] Not in each individual case fully developed form. Think of us imperfect human beings! Also the word "enduring" must not be taken as eternally enduring; only as possessing some degree of continuity beyond the visible.

individual. The faint glow they have carried over into the darkness may serve to call to themselves, by some law of attraction or affinity, all the other attributes they need to fill out the completeness of their quality, so that again they may be part of a manifestation of that quality. This new manifestation may be said to carry within itself not immortality, but the germ of immortality.

This is, of course, pure speculation. It is merely a picture of how personality might grow.

The precise method is purely—perhaps some may say wildly—hypothetical. It is suggested merely as a reasonable possibility; reasonable because in essential process, if not in precise method, it follows every other process we have observed in nature. It represents merely an extension of the premises. It falls within observed laws, and demands for itself the formulation of no new rules or processes, the performance of no "miracles." It is in line with the customary and established procedures that obtain in the rest of observed cosmos.

This becomes plainer if we follow the supposed process a little farther. Out of the X number of attributes necessary to complete any quality let us suppose that three have thus survived as enduring beyond the visible and have become the nucleus of a new being. In time this three will become four, by development either in this or in some other entity. After still another period the four will become five. It is accretion; and probably by a geometrical ratio, for the same originality or persistence or endurance or exuberance or vitality that carried over the original three would in all probability persist, and in continued operation strengthen not only themselves but their associated attributes.

During this process of evolution the individual beings possessing these enduring attributes are nevertheless not in themselves completely continuing. In order that such should after death retain its complete outline, it would have to possess in enduring form all the attributes of its quality. It would not do for it to possess merely $X - I$ of those attributes. If one lacked, it would be supplied from its quality, and the next manifestation of that particular group of attributes would therefore be a mixed, a *new* individual.

But supposing, by happy accident or long focused development, or whatever, some individual did attain enduring completeness of attribute, and died, but nevertheless went on. Would it persist even for a time as a continuing member of its quality? It seems improbable. Why? For the simple reason that it would doubtless have by then acquired potentialities above and beyond the X attributes constituting its present quality. In correspondence it would before its next manifestation have attracted to itself at least one attribute which is not inherent in its former quality of consciousness. Because of that inclusion its quality would now be different. It must embody itself differently. Its sum of attributes, from the standpoint of its former quality, is no longer merely the complete X. It is X plus I. The X qualities demanded an awareness-mechanism in one form. X plus I would demand another awareness-mechanism which will express also the I. That would be a quality above the old quality.

Thus we see, as we should expect, the germ of immortality beginning very far down in the scale; and we see that its development must be slow; and that it must culminate in the completed product only after a long course of evolution. That is in line with other processes in cosmos. It is still a germ. It is not completely personal continuity. It could not be manifested as a continuing creature because it is not yet complete, or anywhere near complete. To become complete it must attract to itself, or have added to itself in the course of evolution, from or by its quality, all the other elements necessary to completeness. And these are both changing, and cf overwhelming majority. There is, to repeat, a germ of continuity, feebly working and growing, but no continuity of the rounded self-contained thing we call an entity.

It must develop and grow, as all other things in the universe develop and grow.

4

When is that? Where can this germ manage to recruit to itself all the elements of completeness in continuing form? With man? or with lower animals than man? 'That is, of course, impossible to say. Nor, do I believe, could it be answered by such a statement as that it begins with, say, horses or dogs or canary birds or anything else. Why not? For the very simple reason that it is personal, individual, not specific. Theoretically, it might begin, *in the one case*, with a horse. And he alone out of all his horse quality might be the only one to have developed—by some happy concatenation—all the elements of consciousness in continuing form. But one could hardly on that account make the general statement that continuity begins with horses;—or dogs—or canary birds!

Or it may be that only in the case of man himself does that completeness of element obtain.

We cannot speak with any assurance on that point, but our mathematical formula may help us to some interesting speculations.

If X is the sum of the continuing attributes acquired by any individual, and Y is the sum of the attributes of consciousness, then X—Y—I is not a continuing complete creature. As soon as it acquires the I it is. Is there any one attribute of consciousness which is obviously the last to be acquired in evolution as we know it? If so the point of acquisition of that attribute in continuing form is quite likely to be the point at which the creature begins as a complete and continuing entity.

It is, of course, difficult to pick out such an attribute. But of them all the altruistic affection we call love seems to us to be at once the highest and the most inclusive of all the qualities of consciousness we know; and since it is the highest, we may presume it to be the last to be acquired in personal and enduring form. The word love is a sticky word with too many connotations of sentimentality, of wishy-washiness, of bestiality, of "sweetness and light," but it is the only word I can find. It must be stripped of those connotations, and understood in its primal simplicity and strength. So understood how would it be to adopt it as a measure in our search for the real personality?

At first glance that seems not so bad a rough definition. We can all distinguish by the feel, as one might say, between beings that have personality and those who have not. It is certainly not the human quality that makes the difference. We all know dogs or cats or horses that are very distinctly "persons," or come mighty near being such;[3] in contrast to swarms of dogs and cats and horses that are simply horses and cats and dogs. The former possess some element of character that the latter lack. This element may very well be the capacity for love.

But the briefest consideration shows us that this will not do. Maternal affection exists well down the scale in specimens where we find no trace of that undefinable but unmistakable personality. Affection for the mate likewise. There are many instances, too, where one can distinguish at least a convincing appearance of purely altruistic action. I have seen, in Central Africa, the hartebeest go out of his way, *and directly into danger,* to arouse members not only of his own but of other species to the fact of my presence. Single members of this species are prone to mount high termite hills in the noon hours, when all the animal world takes its siesta, there to stand as vigilant sentinels. Of course one might

---

[3] I find that some who have read this Mss constantly tend to forget that for immortality it is not sufficient merely to possess an attribute:—that might be only a quality manifestation. It must possess the attribute in personally enduring form.

argue that these are merely exceptionally nervous individuals intent on saving their own skins; but as a matter of fact the sentinels are not always the same, and instances have been observed where one replaces or relieves another who has stood his trick. Wounded elephants are often helped from the field by their comrades. Friendships, having apparently nothing to do with sex or protection, are familiar to us among our domestic animals. But they are also not uncommon among wild beasts. I knew of such a friendship between a wildebeest and a Thompson's gazelle. This incongruous pair dwelt near Kapiti and I had a chance to observe them for several days. They went everywhere together. Sometimes they mingled with a herd of other game, but often they were off by themselves.

All this is love and affection in one form or another. Some of it is particular and individual, as in the cases last mentioned; some of it is partially a specific characteristic, as the hartebeest or the permanent mating of eagles, wild geese, possibly lions; some of it is practically universal, like maternal affection. Love, without further definition, would seem to be too comprehensive.

In all this, however, we can discover one broad principle. The wild animal's affections are directed principally toward his own species. Only rarely, and incidentally, are they directed toward other kinds of animals. The wildebeest and the "Tommy" seem to be merely an interesting exception. The hartebeest's warnings of danger were directed toward his own kind of people—the grazing game. I cannot imagine his bothering with wart hog, for example, or baboons. A great part of this sort of love might be classed as largely instinctive, a part of the wisdom of quality. We speak of the maternal instinct. It is extended and amplified and made personal; it contains the germ; but it is still, in general, inextricably mingled with the instinctive activity that informs the details of everyday life. This, of course, we should expect. Love, too, is an attribute, obtaining by experience its enduring quality.

But in the case of some domesticated animals,—notably the dog— whose opportunities of experience have been much extended by their associations, the relationship of affection is voluntarily extended to include human beings. Much of this relationship, also, we must recognize, is instinctive. It is a heritage of wisdom from the memory and experience of the dog quality. The dog quality has found that it pays to be associated with man. In the remote past, and throughout all the ages since, it has proved to be a profitable partnership. A three-weeks-old puppy, possessed of no wisdom of personal experience at all, will illustrate to anyone's satisfaction. When growled at by some dignified and grouchy patriarch of his own species, he will fly shrieking, not to his mother, but to the nearest human being. His instinct is toward man. And if he grows up to be merely one of a pack, and if it conceivably could happen that he should never come into more than formal relationship with any human being, then his attitude throughout life would remain much the same. He would retain his alliance with man; he would hunt with him, perhaps fight for him; he would remain in his vicinity, and would manifest toward him a sort of loose loyalty in preference to the rest of the animal world. But it would still remain an instinctive affection.

If, on the other hand, as quite often happens, he lives from his early youth in intimate and sympathetic contact with an understanding master, he is capable of astonishing development in personality. This is no place for dog stories, nor is their repetition necessary. One is limited indeed who cannot recollect many individual examples of loyalty, devotion, unselfish love, and at times the highest sacrifice.

I must emphasize the word individual. From even intimate human contact it seems probable that most domestic dogs acquire little more than an accelerated opportunity to develop the birthright they have received from their quality,—to fill out that particular level. But of certain particular exceptions we are accustomed to say, even in common speech, that they are "almost human." It may be that we are not too far from the mark; that in those cases the sum total of personally continuing attributes is approaching the complete Y; that in Y—I the I has almost disappeared.

If I were, then, to attempt, in view of all these considerations, a formulation—which must by its nature be purely speculative—I should cast it about like this:

The soul[4] is born when the individual, of *his own volition*, looks with love not only outside but above himself. In other words, when he makes for himself a god.

That formula must be taken on very broad lines.

It does not attempt to fix an exact point of time.

But it might serve broadly to define a symptom, to act as a marker indicating about the stage of development when we could reasonably expect personal immortality, to indicate approximately when the attributes of the individual seem to have reached the fullness which shall endure. Then the soul is born.

---

[4] The completely continuing personality.

CHAPTER 12

THE REINCARNATION IDEA

~

1

BORN where? born how? we may ask. We cannot answer that; but we can make one positive statement in regard to it. That is, that no individual consciousness can exist without embodiment in substance. There can be no such thing as a "disembodied spirit." Pure spirit is possible only as an infinite thing. When conditioned by space and time any consciousness whatever is inseparable from life and substance. I hope we have made that clear in the first part of this work. So if we are to postulate continuity at all, we cannot escape the truth that every individual consciousness is continuously and at all times possessed of some sort of a body, an awareness-mechanism expressed in substance. Otherwise it instantly ceases to be an individual consciousness and becomes identical with infinite consciousness. The body, as we know, may cease to be the body we have on earth, but it must have substance and be an awareness-mechanism. Furthermore, that body of substance—whatever its constitution and form—must at the moment of death be in possession of the individual consciousness. We cannot conceive the latter leaving the one body and transferring itself to the other. It would suffer obliteration en route.

What the form or constitution may be of this new bodily expression is unknown; or what its powers; or what the environment and correspondences it must meet. We may be certain, however, that it will be an expression of the human quality of consciousness and that it will serve as an awareness-mechanism. It may be an enduring body; or it too, like this earth body, may suffer replacement when the especial conditions to which it is adapted become outgrown or outworn. That does not matter. It may be that upon death we enter fully upon an "immortal" or "spiritual" body, and it may be that we merely come into possession of another temporary affair, like the somewhat decrepit rattletrap we are at present driving. But if we survive, we shall have a body, made out of substance.

2

This, in my belief, is the real basis of the reincarnation idea. Reincarnation, in the generally accepted use of the word, is merely a very specialized way of looking at the same truth. According to it people die and eventually find themselves in possession of a new body, just as we have outlined above; only this new body is the same sort of body again, and it will exist on this same earth. Thus any human soul that has at all developed must have led a long series of lives—such as we know. Some people claim to have been able to recollect fragments of some of their past existences.

The idea is sound at the bottom, and is based on rational grounds. It is very unreasonable to assume that the allotted seventy years should decide a man's status for the rest of his existence. Considering the brevity of time, the limited choice among the multitude of possibilities, and what appears to be a decided lack of the square deal when it comes to luck, opportunity and personal endowment, the contention becomes frivolous. Only a most orthodox and theology bewildered medievalist can honestly and literally, in the depths of his real and not on the surface of his conventional belief, see any sense in that proposition. The injustice, not to say idiocy, of such an arrangement shrieks aloud for at least a modifying corollary. Even the medievalist supplied something of the sort in the shape of arbitrary and inconsequent merciful interpositions. His god was able to "save" any chance miserable sinner—if his mood happened to be right.

The classical reincarnation theory was an attempt to make a modifying corollary not quite so dependent on caprice. By its tenets a man was not bound forever by his performances in one life. He came back to try it again; and yet again until he had learned all there was to be learned, and had all the chances any reasonable man could ask.

The conditions in which he found himself were determined by his previous incarnations. If he had done well, he found himself in favorable circumstances; and if he had done ill, he discovered that he had come down in the world and would have to try again with less in his favor. The adherents of metempsychosis added another and picturesque touch. According to them the hoggish man was quite likely to be reincarnated as a hog.

Now there can be no quarrel with the general principle underlying all this. There is no reason, that we know, why it may not be true in detail. But logic is against quite so narrow an application. There is no question that the soul is "reincarnated" in the sense that it occupies a body of some sort. If it were not, it would, as we have seen, cease to exist. Its germ in the course of development must have been so reincarnated many times. Possibly, perhaps probably, it will in the future find itself in a great variety of developmental surroundings, to each of which an especial or different sort of awareness-mechanism is appropriate. In that case it will also find itself successively possessed of a number of bodies of varying types. Perhaps it may die into these bodies; perhaps one body may merely develop into another. It is not unlikely that for one reason or another some individuals may again find the elements they need for their personal evolution in earth conditions, and so indeed be "reborn" here. All these things fall logically within our framework.

But that the latter should invariably be the case is not so reasonable. It is, I think, only another example of our incurable cosmic provincialism. We always like to think of our little planet as the center of a somewhat extensive visible universe. One of our bitterest historical resentments was against Copernicus for showing that everything did not revolve about us. Indeed, for some time we refused absolutely to believe him, and visited on him that sweet reasonableness which accompanies our disbeliefs. There is no basis whatever, except this provincialism, for assuming that our tiny planet is the only developing ground for quality. We have a great variety of combinations here, to be sure; but they must be nothing to the variety of combinations that exist elsewhere.

And any given quality of consciousness, as we remember, tends to manifest itself where the conditions for it are most suitable. It goes where it finds its need answered. We are here on this earth—unsatisfactory as it seems to many—because it is the sort of thing we need at the present time, disagreeable and unjust and burdensome as it may appear to some. But in infinite possibility it must represent a very small proportion.

Classical reincarnation thus is disclosed to be a half-truth. It may well be that a soul is reborn again and again in one environment. If so, it must be learning slowly. There must, to repeat, be an infinity of possible environments with an infinity of different conditions; sufficient to answer with delicacy the finer adjustments of all possible needs. The reason life manifests itself here rather than there, or there rather than here, is because the individuality that manifests that particular bit of life for the moment needs there rather than here, or here rather than there. And if it cannot fulfil its needs within a reasonable time, perhaps it would do better to change its school!

It would be rather a joke on those people who think they recall a hundred lives on this earth—and are therefore proud of their vast experience—were they to learn that it has been the same experience all the time!

CHAPTER 13

THE STOREHOUSE OF MEMORY

~

1

IT is one thing to possess continuity. From the personal point of view it is quite another to enjoy continuity. It will avail us little, as far as satisfaction goes, if our continuity is divided off into segments which have nothing to do one with the other. If when we leave the physical body we begin an entirely new experience, in complete oblivion of the existence we have left, we might as well be obliterated and be done with it. We must remember. And if we are to rest easy on a rational faith in survival, we must go further and determine whether or not we have reason to believe we shall know anything about it. We must take up the subject of memory.

2

Possibly we have made sufficiently evident the distinction between the two kinds of memory. There was the memory of the quality. of consciousness to which any creature belongs; and there was also the individual memory of that creature. The former was best exemplified by those organisms that work mainly outside of free will. We saw how the millions of experiences of the sand wasp were stored away in the memory of its quality, and were utilized in its accurate instinct in the matter of the caterpillar. That its experiences were actually existent in some body of memory that could be recollected is proved by those very instincts. If they were not stored somehow, in utilizable form, they would be lost. Furthermore, we must conclude that any experience whatever that happens to any creature must touch intimately its quality of consciousness for the simple reason that the creature must be considered as a sense organ, an awareness-mechanism for that quality. And furthermore again, we are justified in the assumption that no memory is ever lost, no matter how insignificant it may be. Given the need, or the proper conditions, it can be "recalled'"—as either a definite mental process or as a structure or an instinct—in complete and clear form.

All but the last of the foregoing propositions we have considered before, and in detail. They are recapitulated here merely to assemble all elements for discussion. That no memory is lost in the body of consciousness is logical. However, we do not have to depend on logic, for it is now established that even in the individual no memory is ever lost. We are all familiar enough with the fact that at times what we wish to recall aggravatingly eludes us; we "cannot put our hand on it"; it "was on the tip of our tongue." And then a little later, when perhaps it has ceased to be of importance, it "pops into our mind"—where it has been all the time. But that this submerged body of memory is complete has only been recently established. Now science tells us that no act, no thought, no word of all our lives is actually gone. It continues to exist in the "subconscious." It may be so deeply buried that no effort of the conscious mind can bring it to recollection. It has as completely vanished, as far as our thinking selves are concerned, as though it had never been. No one can recall his very earliest childhood, for example. There comes a point, as we grope back, where events become isolated, far apart. Finally the mists close and we can remember no farther.

Nevertheless, certain abnormal conditions may in the most unexpected fashion bring to the surface things that otherwise would have remained buried. A shock, great danger, a fever will sometimes do this. All the events of my life flashed before me" is a familiar phrase. This has long been understood. It may be favorably observed in the case of the supernormal psychology of sensitiveness or mediums. There is the classical often quoted instance of the girl who, while in trance, made long speeches in Greek, a language with which she was personally totally unfamiliar. It subsequently developed that many years before she had been in the employ of a learned man who, for his own pleasure, used to declaim aloud sonorous passages from Homer and the Greek dramatists. This fact the girl claimed had slipped her mind. Whether it had or not is unimportant. The point is that the Greek itself, in all its variety and richness, had for many years remained in her submerged memory, and could be recalled intact by appropriate procedure. Hypnotic experiment has led the mind back and back in a most convincing manner. It would be interesting to conduct a series of such experiments to determine in the first place just how far back into infancy the memory could be led; and in the second place to see whether that memory would not be found to begin with the commencement of a certain type of experience. It seems to me probable that it would be found co-temporaneous with the first activity of the free will.

The point we are making was many years ago strikingly exemplified in an incident that came under my own notice. I was rooming in Paris with a young man who was very suddenly and very deeply disappointed in love. He took it well during his waking hours; but when he went to bed he entered a state of disassociated consciousness, which lasted generally two or three hours before he fell into normal sleep. During this condition he talked. His talk was an exact reproduction, not only in words, but in inflection and loudness, of things he had said in his past life. He began invariably with early childhood and worked slowly down to the present, reproducing typical scenes of each age. By means of the exact words and exclamations he had used he reconstructed a hundred trivial incidents. It was like listening to one end of a telephone conversation. I had known the man for many years, and I was able to verify the astounding literal accuracy of the performance in hearing again his end of conversations we had had together, and which I myself had utterly forgotten until thus given the cue. Each evening a different series of incidents was selected. Nearly always they were unimportant; and in most cases, as I found by inquiry, had passed from the man's conscious memory completely. Yet here they were, as though from a phonograph record, with even the little chuckles accurately reproduced.

There is already a considerable literature on the subject, which has been named cryptomnesia. It all goes to show, astonishing as the fact may seem, that nothing is forgotten or lost.

3

Since this is provably so of the individual, the same thing may be predicated for quality memory.

In consciousness in general must exist all things that have been experienced.

The memory content of an individual must necessarily, then, be a mixed sort of thing. Any person, as we have seen, retains as part of his own possession everything that he himself has done or thought or experienced. He also falls heir to a proportion of this quality memory. He has certain "instincts," which are a direct heritage from the race as a race. He has also certain bodily organs or functions and automatic reflexes and the like which are the direct result of experience and experiment, and wisdom thereby acquired, by the human consciousness-quality. Those are examples of memory possession on the lower degrees.

And, conversely, man undoubtedly undergoes certain experiences which have more to do with his quality than with himself; and which enter directly the quality-memory, passing his individual memory by. They are his only as he is part of the human quality. We do not in any sense of the word remember, as individuals, the intricate experiences we underwent in digesting our food a year ago; and yet those experiences may have had a powerful effect on some adaptations, through quality, going on in the human system. The human physical structure is daily undergoing thus a multitude of experiences having to do with the sensorial and instinctive, and therefore automatic, end of the spectrum. These alterations and adaptations may in time modify or change something in the structure of future human beings, but they have only slight influence on the individual's own final structure. A great many of these experiences, such as the beating of the heart, are beyond conscious control, and equally beyond individual memory.

Nevertheless, they enter the store of quality memory and are available to the "likes of us." A great deal of this storehouse of memory is at least partly open to us. We are constantly using it subconsciously, and to a small extent consciously.

We are continually "remembering" from that store. Every time we take a breath, we are remembering the moment when, urged by mounting exuberance of life, we crawled out on the shore of some primordial sea. All our bodily functions, all our delicate physical adjustments are memories of long past experiences, of trials and errors, and failures, and trials again.

But we must not lose sight of the fact that this structural and more or less automatic type of memory is only a small portion of what our human quality has experienced and must remember. The merely physical life is, and for a long time has been, a relatively unimportant minority in the sum of human existence. There is, in the correspondence to this higher life, a body of memory which, like the memory of the body functions, should be more or less available to every individual.

Indeed, it is available, but to a very limited extent. We have a capricious and unruly command of it. This is not astonishing when we reflect upon how little we remember and utilize even of the experiences of our individual lives. Very few people can recall the details of any one day twenty years ago. Yet there is no doubt that we should be a great deal wiser than we are if we could remember and utilize all the deeds of our days, as my friend in Paris remembered. If we, with our especial brain equipment, and our practice and incentive of daily living, and our memory and systems of different sorts can do so little with what has actually happened to us personally, it is not surprising that we do considerably less with what is only dimly and partially to be perceived in the best of circumstances.

Nevertheless, we do manage to touch it at times. We touch intuition—erratically: we have inspirations,—rare, and not to be commanded. These things are quality wisdom drawn from quality memory of race experience. They are recollections, seized almost at random it seems, and yet with often a correspondence to need so beautiful that one could with difficulty avoid the thought of a personal and beneficent supervision. There may be such supervision for all I know; but I conceive that if such be the case the aid extended must be a directing of natural currents, so to speak. A lack in a human soul must, to the extent of its equipment, tend to draw to itself from its human quality of consciousness, as a magnet draws only its affinity from a heap of mixed filings, that which will complement it.

Sometimes, in rare and apparently accidental cases, someone appears to dip into this body of memory in a more concrete form. We have all experienced the sudden shock of feeling, though in a strange place, that we have "been there before." Usually this is merely a generalized impression, but occasionally it becomes definite. A friend of mine once happened upon an obscure little valley in Switzerland which carried with it this sense of familiarity. Before entering it he described for the benefit of his companions exactly what would be found there. A great deal was precisely as he described; but there were certain discrepancies, the most important of which was that in one spot where he predicted a pine forest lay an open farm. However, careful research verified all his details, including the forest, as existing fifty years before. My friend had never been abroad, and knew nothing of this particular valley. It was a striking, but by no means unique example of this type of recollection.

The Society for Psychical Research has verified and recorded many of them. The feats of psychometry—the reading of facts from an object held in the hand are in my view in the same category; that is, a more or less accidental contact with what exists in the memory of the larger consciousness of which we—and everything else—are a part.

Another friend visited our household who possessed the latter mysterious power to a marked degree. Blindfolded she would take between her palms small objects I would select, whose history I alone knew, and whose very nature were concealed from her by their wrappings or the way they were folded or what not. Without moving her palms she would name the object, give an account of the high lights of its history, and even at times describe accurately the characteristics of persons unknown to her who had something to do with the object. This experiment was repeated again and again with things of all sorts from all parts of the world. The proved explanation must of course be as yet obscure; but the facts of the matter could not be questioned. Many hypotheses are possible. Telepathy might be one of them; but in that case it would be of a highly selective type. And in some experiments she was given one of many similar objects at random whose exact identity I did not myself know until *after* her statements.

It seems more reasonable to me that here, as I have said, through some aptitude and by some process as yet unknown to us—including herself—she gained a partial command of the type of race or quality memory we have been discussing. It also seems reasonable that this may be a faculty in embryo, so to speak, a foreshadowing of a power that may with development expand to the point of conscious command, at least to a certain extent. Such command must lie far in the future of the race, but it appears a logical extension in evolution. Our powers are as yet feeble, but in some directions definitely adumbrated. In the highest conceivable development we might even imagine an individual conscious entity able to touch and use at will this venerable wisdom, these many experiences both of successes and of failures, this store of memories extending back through the whole history not only of a race but of a type of consciousness. In comparison our own little submerged individual memory fades into insignificance.

4

In all this we see in reality two processes: one the storing of experience in memory; the other the recollection of required details, the bringing them to the surface of consciousness. All the memories always exist, as long as the entity to which these things have happened continues to exist; but they are not all and always available. Certain sets of circumstances are necessary to make them available. Sometimes these circumstances are the result of conscious effort, as when we put our minds to "remembering" a thing; sometimes they are the result of chance, as when a stray perfume arouses—acutely things forgotten; sometimes they are the result of supernormal or abnormal conditions, as in the case of the hypnotized or of the medium in trance. But they are always brought to light because of the gathering of certain conditions. Many of them would not, in the regular course of events, have come to the surface at all. It required the unusual or unexpected or abnormal circumstances to arouse them. Nevertheless, always, when they are so aroused, they are found to be unblurred, fresh in their pristine perfection.

They have suffered no tarnishing, no deterioration in their long submerges. My Paris friend's abnormal recollection was as exact of the most trivial details of his early childhood as of the events of that very day.

Thus it is entirely conceivable, even most probable, that for each memory, for every one of the innumerable minutiae hidden in the subconscious, some one particular and appropriate set of circumstances must exist fitted for its evocation. All that is needed for its recollection is a knowledge of just what that set of circumstances may be.

5

It seems to me probable that the storehouse of memory is not primarily dependent on the physical brain cells; but that the mechanism of evocation at the present moment is. The brain cells are a perishable institution; while, as we have seen, the memory storehouse is co-terminus with the individual. It is part of his substance; can never be lost; exists as long as he exists. It is a part of consciousness; and consciousness continues.

But the power of recollection to the conscious mind in this physical life is intimately connected with the brain. Disease, or a blow on the head, Or a surgical operation can quite destroy this power. We are familiar, in fiction and in life, with the man who suddenly loses all memory of himself and takes up a new life of perhaps an entirely different nature from the old. It may last for years, and then another rap on the skull brings him back to his former existence. The two existences have absolutely no recollection, and hence no knowledge, one of the other. As far as the bystander is concerned it has been the same man throughout, the same continuing individual As far as he personally is concerned, however, his beginning and appreciation of himself as in the second phase dates from the accident. As far as his former self is concerned, he is obliterated. Then when the second blow brings him back to his former state his continuity subjectively is (a) his life before the first accident, and (b) his life after the second accident. Everything between a and b is as though it never was. That personality is now obliterated.

Nevertheless, we know that the memories of all experiences in both existences do exist in his submerged mind. An appropriate set of conditions can, often does, evoke some of them. If the modification produced in the brain by the falling brick could be applied with skill and sufficient knowledge, it is quite in line that he could come into possession of both experiences.

This is a very good example of interrupted continuity. Another we experience every day of our lives when we fall asleep. There is then also a blank that separates two distinct epochs of existence. It is so habituated a phenomenon that we take it for granted. It never seems to us that we might deny a continuity of personality merely because we have lost a portion of it. We have no waking recollection of what memories we may have stored during those hours. We have no knowledge of them at all, nor whether or not we have stored any memories. Nor, in those hours of rest, have we any recollection of our days. The one throws on the other but faint shadows of dreams.

We have then a huge storehouse of latent memory, and a mechanism for evoking a very small proportion of that memory. The mechanism is, like all other mechanisms with which we are provided, adapted to its job. It evokes what we need and what we can utilize. We would be overwhelmed were all these things we possess, or even a very small percentage of them, permitted to beat for attention on our conscious minds. The bewilderment would render us impotent. We have available, and we use, just the kind and variety, and in general the quality of conscious memories that our particular environment requires. An entirely comatose consciousness would use no memories at all. A reawakening consciousness would use memories just to the extent of its awakening. A man recovering from a blow remembers first of all merely to breathe, then to move in fear of pain, then perhaps to thirst.

As he comes to, as he occupies more life, he uses more and more, until at length he is, as we say, in full possession of his faculties.

6

It would be an act of daring to attempt to define the limits of the physical brain as an evoking mechanism from the submerged memory. Yet, in spite of isolated cases that hint rather than prove to the contrary, I am tempted to define them as the limits of physical life. It is adapted to this earth and its conditions, and it is capable of functioning in that environment. That is what it is for. True, there seem to have been instances when recollection has apparently extended either beyond this present life or beyond an individual personality. These incidents may or may not have been real. Assuming their authenticity, it seems to me more likely that they were called up by some other apparatus than the brain, perhaps by some adumbration of a mechanism that will reach its perfection in some other state of consciousness. The brain is in structure physical, and in this respect would seem to have to do with physical things.

And from that we are justified, I believe, in a generalization. The mechanism of evocation to the conscious mind from the submerged storehouse of memory is a mechanism for the construction of the proper circumstances for recollection of memory. *That mechanism is the one which fits the need of the entity in the life to which it is called.*

7

Then, if we admit individual conscious survival, we must sooner or later conceive that the entity will come into possession of some such mechanism. If it moves at all, it must be able to utilize some memory. Otherwise it is completely comatose. The number of memories it can use depends entirely on how much it moves, or is capable of moving. In other words, one's command of memory depends entirely on the degree of expansion, on the radius of life one can occupy.

The question of the degree of memory after death, then, is as to what use one can make of it. It may be that, as we have done here, we shall make a fresh start, without recollection of our former state. But even in that case, sooner or later, if we continue to grow and expand and reach out, we are going to be able to utilize to advantage more and more of the memories from our storehouse. There must, reasonably, come a time when we shall be justified, when our need demands, in the use of memories from a previous state of existence. And once that happens, instantly a sense of continuity is established between those two states of existence.

It might be rather a feeble and partial sense at first, but it would increase as one increased his Capacity to use. Expansion of consciousness would make more and more widely available more and more of what consciousness has laid away. As it grew it would be able to use a greater and greater proportion from its storehouse, reaching farther and farther back in its previous existence. At the last it might be able to utilize at least portions from all states of its existence, and so become possessed of a complete and conscious continuity.

From these considerations we see inspiringly that, like everything else beyond the small free gift of life and ready-made instincts, the sense of continuity as well as continuity itself is a growing thing and a thing that must be earned.

CHAPTER 14

NATURE'S BLIND GENIUS

~

1

I N the last chapter we casually mentioned 'the small free gift of life and ready-made instincts." What may we mean by that?

We have become accustomed—mainly because of long reiteration—to consider a state of nature as nearly synonymous with perfection. Man "falls away from a state of nature" to his own detriment. His attention is constantly called to the marvelous devices and processes of nature, with the added advice that he can do no better than to imitate them. Nature represents the smooth and beautiful working of a harmony which man's blundering efforts tend to nullify. Sentimental philosophers have drawn for us a primitive figure from whose perfectness they tell us we have "fallen." Theologians have emphasized that proposition.

As a matter of fact, the natural order, as we see it, is marvelously, stupendously ingenious in its adaptations, but it is often stupid in its methods. Viewed as the result of a development through the medium of thousands of experimental developments it transcends any praise we could tell of it; viewed as a thing designed for a specific purpose,—as a machine is designed, *ab initio*,—it is very faulty.

Why should not this be so? Nature, in the case of any particular organism, has reached her end through a long evolution of experiments. A great many of these experiments have been discarded; others have been utilized for a while and have been outgrown and displaced by a better device; still others exist only as vestigial remains, which may—like the appendix—even prove troublesome. Nature works in old material—both of substance and of idea. She does the best she can with it. That best is almost incredibly ingenious. The deeper our studies into the "web of life," the more profound our admiration of this ingenuity, of the relations and interrelations that result in attaining the desired end.

But considered all by itself the system is often inept. Given merely the idea of the thing, and permission to make a fresh start with any materials or processes he might please to select out of the whole bag of tricks, any intelligent person could often devise a simpler and better method of getting the same final result.

The process of producing the human being is a case in point. Looked at closely in detail, we can feel nothing but wonder at its ingenuity from start to finish. From the moment the male cell moves with fairly an intelligent energy in its search for the ovum; through the long and complicated period of gestation in which by ingenious chemical devices the cells first are differentiated into various functions, and then are enabled to select from the mother's blood the elements appropriate to each, to the moment when remarkable physical adaptations in the mother's very structure permit birth, and equally remarkable expedients bridge the transition from the parasitic to the wholly independent creature, these involved processes are fitted together in a mutual adaptation that is nothing less than amazing. *Considering the material she had to work with, and considering the already-made conditions she had to meet,* Nature has done a remarkable job. But taken all by itself we cannot say much for it. It is a poor piece of mechanics,—wasteful of time, wasteful of energy; a cause of suffering; dangerous; in short plain stupid. About its only real recommendation is that it does produce the child.

The same may be said of many other devices and functions of the human body; as also of many of the devices and functions of the universe about us. A typhoon or a cyclone are blunderings incidental to the very ingenious meteorological balance. Everywhere we see ends reached by marvels of adroit compromises and balances which in themselves are our admiration and despair. The intelligence of their complicated interplay is stupendous. Yet considered each one by itself they are often both clumsy and wasteful.

Why not? If we conceived of all cosmos as a system called into being at a stroke, we could legitimately wonder at such discrepancies and desperate expedients. But when we consider that the whole thing is a growing self-awareness of finite consciousness itself, a slow differentiation of that consciousness into its qualities, then we begin to see reason in it all. Nature has not only to fit her new things to her old things, but she must make her new things out of her old things; her new ideas grow out of her old ideas. She is not only evolving new expedients, but she is constantly engaged in suppressing old ones that are either unsuccessful or outgrown, but which nevertheless still retain an influence on the interplay. Her experiments in reproduction have been made in many different ways: simple division of cells, production of spores, external planting of seeds, and so on in a ceaseless groping toward what will fulfil not only all requisites of reproduction of species, but also of innumerable psychic relations and dependencies. She is still far from ideal perfection, but she has even in an acknowledgedly clumsy method already gained permanently certain essentials.

In many of these organs and functions which do quite closely approximate efficiency we can still observe the remains of former experiments—or intermediary successes—which nature has discarded but whose traces she has not quite erased. Hair on the human body is not only practically useless but detrimental. It has no longer value as a clothing; it tends to harbor dirt and microbes; it is favorable to certain skin diseases. The shape of our ears suggests the megaphone catching of sound, but is in reality of no use in that respect. We have still seven muscles that used to move this ear trumpet about—like a horse—*when it was still of value*, but which now are useless. The pulp in the corner of the eye is of no use whatever. It was an experiment which we can see fully carried out in the "third eyelid" of the bird. The appendix was an experiment in nutrition. In the earliest vegetarian mammals it was a large sac in which the coarse food was broken up by bacteria. There are 107 such vestigial remains in the human body alone. They exist as vestigial remains because of the fact of evolution. When consciousness found a better idea than the appendix sac for breaking up food, it could not build the new idea into form from fresh materials, so to speak. It had to take the old machine and modify it in accordance with the new plan. The pituitary gland is a curious example of the use of old material for an entirely different purpose. It was originally a supposed cyclops eye.

So, as we see, it does not necessarily mean that the old idea was wholly abandoned. On the contrary it is extremely probable that in some form of life it was itself carried—or is being carried—to as near perfection as is possible. All about us we see that. Some individual species represent or embody their own idea much better than we could possibly represent that idea, for all our advanced intelligence and development. We have not yet succeeded in cooperating as the bees cooperate; nor in governing ourselves as well as do the ants. There are plenty of things we have not been able to do as well as they have been done in nature. When we find out how to construct as light yet as rigid a flying apparatus as is the head of a ripe dandelion, we will do some real air navigation.

When we understand and acquire the sense of direction of migrating birds, we shall never get lost. All through evolution we see this perfection of the idea; and then the passing on to construct something more elaborate on the basis of the last. Everything is becoming.

2

In all this series we note several general principles.

The first is that the older the form, the more nearly it seems to express its own idea and to fit with its surroundings. It has reached the end, or nearly the end, of its evolution. There are not many more improvements to make, so far as it is concerned.

The second is that such nearly perfected creatures act by instinct almost entirely. Intelligence Or initiative has very little to do with their daily existence. As individuals they are born with a ready-made equipment for life.

The third is that the few and simple things they are called upon to do are most admirably done. We never get over marveling at the powers of intelligent action exhibited by such creatures. The books of Henri Fabre are full of instances,—the Emperor moth, the spiders, the wasps and cicadas and crickets of his French dooryard have furnished him with a library of fascinating material. The lower forms of life have a beautiful precision that the upper forms lack.

3

Why is all this so; and what does it mean?

Sentimentalists, of course, tell us that it means a fall from grace, a degeneration. If, say they, man had continued to live a sweet and pure and natural life; if he had not dulled his senses and his mind with an artificial civilization; if he had taken example from the primitive and the feral, then he, too, would still have the power to live in complete harmony with nature. This view was carried to its absurdity by the French school of a century ago. We have considerably receded from their position since, but there is still a considerable residue of the idea left in the minds of many of us. To Rousseau's "noble savage" we vaguely refer at least a modicum of simpler saner living, and certainly a higher ideal of bodily health. The idea will not hold water, even as to bodily health. The savage is not healthier than the civilized man. He is sick quite as often, he ages in fewer years, he dies sooner. If he possesses any advantages at all, they must lie on the side of certain relatively unimportant instinctive powers.

And that is exactly what we should expect. In the very simplest qualities of consciousness experience seemed to come to them through their individual manifestations wholly by chance. Only after considerable evolution had taken place—after the memory of a great many chance experiences had resulted in modification of the Idea—was the individual able even in the smallest way to make his own contribution of experiment. Up to that point all his actions or reactions in life had been absolutely determined for him by his quality wisdom. He had at birth a full ready-made equipment. But pretty far down in the scale, as we remember, some especially vital individual did manage to contribute something of its own; and that point we defined as the real beginning of the individual as a person and not merely as a separate thing. This contribution of experiment was almost infinitesimal in proportion to the ready-made instinctive correspondences of life. Furthermore, it was in all probability blundering and awkward as compared to the smooth perfections of its other and instinct-ordered activities.

This thought gives us a clue. If we look farther, we will see that we have come upon a principle that will apply. *As consciousness rises in evolution the field of the precise instinctive action is narrowed, and the field of the reasoned—and blundering—experimental action is widened.*

4

In other words, any creature is permitted the opportunity to experiment on his own,—and at his own cost, so to speak—in proportion to his development. It is at once a privilege and a responsibility. The first requisite is that he survive and continue his race. His ready-made equipment of instinct is largely devoted to assuring these results. If there is any capacity left over, as one might say, it may be occupied by intelligent effort.

Now intelligent effort is the effort directed mainly by the knowledge and wisdom of the single individual, whose experience and memory are naturally much limited as compared to the experience and memory of his quality of consciousness. It cannot, per se, have the same accuracy as pure instinctive action. But it can have a wider fling., Of course it is helped out to a certain extent by instinct. In the lower forms one might say that intelligent action is conditioned by instinct. On the other hand, individual intelligent action meddles with, modifies instinctive action, sometimes to its detriment. To a degree the sentimentalist has been right. If we could follow pure instinct implicitly, without mussing it up by our personal ideas, we would undoubtedly do what we did do very much better. *But we would do very much less than we do now, and we would never do any more.*

Thus when we rise in the scale to a contemplation of mankind, we find that the instincts are reduced to a bare minimum, and the privilege and duty of experiment—and hence of blunder—largely preponderate. His ready-made equipment has been cut down to just enough to permit of self-preservation. His instincts are not as commanding; and he is constantly modifying their behests according to his own ideas. The outcome is more often than not unsuccessful; and it attains the invariable result of unsuccessful or fragmentary experiment,—discomfort. But he has the privilege and responsibility of an ever larger contribution of experience to his human quality of consciousness. And this in turn, by due process of synthesis,—just as the sand wasp obtained its delicate technique,—will in time help toward a wider instinctive wisdom, an improved ready-made equipment for his own successors. This ready-made equipment will probably be in the line rather of more instinctive potentialities of intuition than of more merely physical instincts.

5

If it is permissible to extend our straight lines forward as well as back, we may make several interesting speculations. In all of evolution up to man we have found that the tendency is to a narrowing of the instinctive field and a widening of the field of intelligent personal equipment. The ready-made equipment for the life history of the ant or the Emperor moth is pretty complete. Whatever comes up, they have a set of blueprints to fit the situation. In all conditions normally to be expected they get on beautifully. Abnormal conditions are successfully met only to a certain extent. Completely unusual conditions are fatal. The personal effort to compass them is feeble. As consciousness becomes more complex, the ready-made equipment is reduced. All the detailed exigencies of life are not covered by the blueprints, only the broader outlines. The creature has advanced enough so that it can be trusted to do a few of the minor adaptations on its own account. Its efforts are not only valuable in its own development, but they add to the experience and memory of its quality of consciousness. It makes a larger and larger proportion of its own life. When we come to mankind, we find him making almost all of his life. A large part of his ready-made equipment consists of his body and his bodily instincts. The rest of the job is mostly his.

Is it not likely that this shifting of proportion will continue? If so, it seems probable that in the further development of consciousness he will find his ready-made portion—on the merely physical side—still more limited, and he will find his opportunity for original construction still further extended. It might even be in some manifestation—either future or elsewhere—the human quality might make its own body, so to speak!

Or to amuse ourselves with another extension, quite logical, but of course purely speculative: We see in all the ascending consciousness of evolution the experience and memory of one quality utilized in the succeeding and more elaborate forms. The hard-won effort of blundering individual experiment does eventually result in something. That something is utilized in forming the ready-made equipment of higher orders. In the sure instinct of one creature we see correlated and digested and synthesized the blunders and successes of those below it in the scale. Perhaps our own original experiments or adaptations of life,—as far as they are successful even to the degree of meeting conditions somehow,—may aid in the ready-made equipment of something beyond our ken.

CHAPTER 15

FREE WILL

~

1

WE have rounded the corner to find ourselves up against the involved and contentious question of free will. If a creature is to make a contribution which we can call original, it must do so by the exercise of choice. If there is no choice, then the contribution is the gift of pure circumstance. And choice, of course, implies freedom of will to at least the extent necessary to make it.

But when first we look upon the web of life with discriminating eyes, we are not so sure. There are complicated dependencies. John Jones thinks he exercised nothing but his own sovereign judgment when he turned down Smith's proposal. As a matter of fact he did so because at the moment his mood inclined toward the pessimistic rather than the optimistic side. He was so inclined because he had been annoyed too soon after breakfast. He was annoyed because the streetcar on which he went to his office crashed into a delivery wagon, and his name had been taken as a witness. That he was on the streetcar at all was due to the fact that it was three minutes behind its schedule and overtook him at a moment of indecision whether he should walk to his office or not. Its appearance tipped the decision. It was three minutes late because a flea stopped a dog in the middle of the tracks and just at the wrong moment. Furthermore, the delivery wagon came along exactly in time to be smashed into because the driver had decided to take the east side first this morning instead of the west side, as was his usual habit; and that decision also had a long train of cause. Now if Jones had accepted Smith's offer he would have made some money and would not have been forced by lack of means to move from his present habitation; in which event his wife who was sick abed at the time would probably have been burned to death when the defective wiring of the house he had been living in got in its deadly work. Ever after Jones pointed to this escape as providential.

Each action of each moment, thus, has a complicated ancestry and equally complicated results. The mind becomes bewildered when it attempts to follow back this genealogy even a dozen steps. The interplay is so intricate, the web of life so woven together, that it becomes impossible that anything should happen but the thing that did happen. And yet at any point in the long sequence it appears that the shift of a hair would have changed the fate not only of the individual but of whole communities. The amazing interdependence has been many times expressed not only in fiction but in proverb. The kingdom lost because of the lack of a horseshoe nail is one. Dusany used the idea strikingly in a play called *If*. The delay of half a minute in catching a particular train makes the difference whether a man ekes out a humdrum life as a suburbanite, or lives splendidly as an Oriental despot.

It is no wonder, when one considers thoughtfully all this, that some minds become sufficiently bewildered to take refuge in fatalism. The human midge is caught in the web of life, and it is useless for him to struggle. Every act of every moment is foreordained. What happens must happen. That he does struggle, in spite of his cynical knowledge of its ultimate uselessness, is itself part of the thing ordained!

2

But this attitude overlooks one consideration. To be sure we may acknowledge that the situation is prepared, and it is prepared inexorably as far as the person confronting it is concerned. To be sure, a very slight shift—which at the time may have been under the decision of someone— would in the past have produced, perhaps, an entirely different situation, or would have presented the same situation under an entirely different aspect. To that extent the thing is out of a man's control.

The actual decision of the moment, however, is his. Furthermore, the kind of decision he will make he has determined for himself by the decisions he has made in the past. Jones allowed annoyance to form his judgment as to Smith's offer. If he had walked to the office and got his lungs full of fresh air, he would probably have accepted it. But, if, in the past, he had, by decisions, gained the ability to remain unaffected by surface mood, the train of circumstances we have detailed would have had no effect on this particular matter at all. As for his wife being burned to death, possibly the money he would have made through Smith would have encouraged him to move to a bigger house.

Therein lies the escape from fatalism. The past has prepared the conditions with which man is confronted. His own history has prepared his own tendencies. But the moment is his own. At that point he can, by his own effort, break with the past. By whatever of fresh impetus, fresh resolve, fresh inspiration he may receive or can command he has the opportunity of transcending himself. And through the fact of that transcendence he commands the future. His moment turns the current here and there, fixing the conditions perhaps for beings yet unborn, just as decisively as some small past unconsidered trifle has placed him in the suburbs or in Teheran.

It also, of course, fixes certain conditions for himself in the future, with which in due time he will be confronted. What they maybe he is not prophet enough even vaguely to guess. He cannot determine whether they may be more or less advantageous, more or less pleasant. All he can be sure of is that they will be different. From his own judgment he is not justified in attempting to forecast very far; and even a short range prophecy is more likely than not to be falsified by other ill-considered but tremendous trifles of which he can know nothing. The present moment is his, and that is all.

Since this is so, and cannot be otherwise, it behooves him to gain, as far as he may, an intrinsic standard of action—a standard that relies on itself irrespective of results. It behooves him also to arouse in himself a live and vital desire which will not permit him without consideration to go in the direction of the obviously prepared. He must act primarily from the vantage ground of his own ethics, and only secondarily from the point of view of results. That is not morality: it is common sense. Also he must cultivate aliveness; so that he does not necessarily follow the line events or moods or contributing conditions have laid out. That may be the best line; but again it may not. That, too, is common sense. When he appreciates these two points, he has gone far to escape the preordination bugaboo, and to take as much command of his destiny as his present powers will permit.

3

This command is limited, in a way, but it is sufficient, and can be extended. It is a genuine command. Individual free will is the authority to take charge of one's own life in whatever conditions may confront it, instead of leaving that charge solely to the quality of consciousness.

From the moment it is gained, in however limited a form, development is accelerated, for it now consists of the experience one gets in running the bit of cosmos under his control. It is a privilege, an order of knighthood. It is a recognition of that capacity for exuberance, for doing new things, which in the beginning made for new qualities in consciousness and fresh species on earth.

It is also a tremendous responsibility. Possessed of it no creature can longer live all of his life comfortably within the instinctive wisdom given it by its quality of consciousness. Something is expected of it. That something varies, of course, according to capacity, whether among the lower creatures or among humans. One sees an opportunity; another does not. The expectation is according to the equipment.

But that part of it, I conceive, is a good deal like natural hunger. The capacity brings with it a desire for fulfilment of it. The desire is sometimes—perhaps most often—smothered by inertia and habit; but it exists as an original accompaniment. It is the urge toward growth we hear so much about.

4

We are glib enough in our talk of free will, as though it were a thing that came to us ready to use, and perfectly rustless and untarnishable. As a matter of fact it is a capacity like any other. It requires development, it requires use. It grows with exercise; it atrophies from disuse. It requires as careful tending as any other delicate faculty in our personal engine. Clogged with carbon of laziness or *laissez-faire* or inertia it runs imperfectly or not at all. In our present state of development our wills are rarely free. They are bound and gagged, cramped, paralyzed and unworkable. What we think is free will is more often a kind of headlong impetus acquired from the pressure of past events and directing itself unmodified by any real personal direction. Free will cannot work until we shake off the predominating influence of these pressures. Free will cannot work until we are free. The body of free volition is the measure of our strength.

By and large an Intelligence of practical omniscience, as far as the physical universe goes, and with the ability to trace out not only immediate but remote causes and effects, could prophesy the future with considerable assurance. Starting from this moment such an Intelligence could map out exactly what is going to happen. He could predict just what Jones or Smith would do a year from today at the hour of ten in the morning. He could in a more general way trace the trend of larger events. Those things will come out precisely as he prognosticates *provided* Smith or Jones or some individual near enough in the web of life to affect them does not rise to a decisive exercise of real free will. And that event is sufficiently rare. The average of human beings follow the sequence. What appears to them an original and unaffected decision has an ancestry of subtleties that make it natural and inevitable unless a definite spiritual effort is made to transcend it. Even the apparently unimportant and capricious trifles of decision, the idle and purposeless followings of a mood, have their remote and tangled origins. We imagine we decide to turn to the right, but it is the current that turns us. We do not feel—are unaware of—the current.

So our supposed Intelligence could acquire considerable of a reputation as a prophet by banking on this inertia. He could at least equal the Weather Bureau as Old Probability. In the possession of free will we have the power of choosing. And one of the choices must be as to whether or not we shall use that power. Indeed, that is the first choice of all.

5

Like everything else, free will must be considered as a product of evolution, beginning with the simple and expanding to the complex. Its earliest phases must be scarcely more than suggestions of, germs of, itself. Whether it, in germ, is co-terminus with immortality, as a germ, is beside the point. That view is alluring, and may be true.

But well down in the scale we find at least the appearance of a certain degree of free will. When an ant chances head on against a pebble he seems to have quite a free choice as to whether he shall go to the right or left of it, or climb over To be sure it may well be that subtle reactions which we cannot trace determine the matter; some delicate influences may touch buttons which bring response from mechanics constructed by quality-wisdom in answer to quite other needs.

An infinitesimal difference in temperature, an angle of light, an imperceptible current of air striking the insect's physical organism may force the decision. But when, on the other hand, we take the trouble to remember that these creatures are provably able to meet fresh conditions and to modify themselves and their actions in accordance; when we reflect that somewhere down here there is occasional instance of individual original contribution to quality of consciousness, then we find it exceedingly difficult to deny such creatures an allotment of at least the beginnings of free will. They have a certain small charge of their own lives.

That free will can be exercised only within a small circle. It is limited to a few things very close at hand. The circumference is uncrossable. Indeed, we soon find that the lower down in the scale we go the more contracted is this circumference. And, conversely, as we go up in the scale, we find the circle within which free will works constantly expanding. As life mounts in the evolution of its qualities, its creatures possess a wider and wider field within which they can do as they like. From this point of view growth may be defined as the enlargement of that circle.

But whether the germ of free will and the germ of immortality are co-temporaneous or not, it seems permissible to define their full acquisition in terms of one another. The germ of free will may be said to become the thing itself when it has so far developed as to carry with it as an attribute the knowledge of good and evil between which to choose. Into the terms of good and evil I have no intention of reading a conventional moral sense. Good is what works in harmony; evil is what works against harmony. The knowledge of good and evil is merely a perception, very dim and wavering at best, of the difference between going in harmony and dour despairful struggle against the rush of life. When the circle within which free will can work has expanded to make this inclusion, then it has become our enduring property and the tool of an immortality.

This is the real free will. It is the gift which at the birth of the soul the Fairy Godmother bestows—as a weapon by which progress may be won, or as a black curse by which its very existence may be destroyed. Heretofore the ordering of the climb has been in the hands of nature.

Henceforward it must be man's own.

Like all the newborn, the soul must be a feeble thing at first. It must be fostered and cherished, or it might expire. But behind it, as behind all other creatures of consciousness, is its quality and all the garnered wisdom her myriad experiences have distilled into the instincts of the race. The abundance of its quality swaddles it about, guarding and warding it until it has gained the strength to grasp. Then in all justice she may demand that the soul in turn shall, by its consciously directed effort, gain its own abundance, in order that it may return to her manifold what it has received; in order that those souls yet unborn or feebly struggling in the first stirrings of life may in their turn have abundance from which to draw. If it fail, it might be destroyed. And it would be destroyed were there not others to make up its deficiencies.

Such is the opportunity and the responsibility of free will.

CHAPTER 16

THE SUBCONSCIOUS WASTEBASKET

~

1

PROGRESS, among other things, is gained by experience and memory. The free will is one of the tools by which we work. Intelligence is another. The mind—in the case of human beings— is the aspect of Intelligence that seems the most important to us. The science of the mind, or psychology, in its purely scholastic definition, has of late years taken on increasing significance, and has made wonderful progress.

As compared with twenty years ago, our knowledge of what goes on inside of our heads, and how it goes on, is comprehensive and illuminating. But for all that psychology is one of the newer sciences. It, like all new sciences, must first determine its terminology. It has been busy largely in observing things and naming things. That is all right, for it is necessary first of all to name things; but the error of considering a thing explained merely because it is named must be very carefully guarded against. Expressing a new mystery in terms of an old mystery is a consoling device. The old mystery is more familiar and so we think we know more about it. The two may even be made interchangeably to "explain" each other. There is an amusing French example of this. One school says, 'What is there astonishing in manifestations under hypnotism? Analogous spontaneous occurrences are known in hysteria." Which of course explains hypnotism because we are more familiar with hysteria. But at the same time another school of thought is declaring; "Why marvel at hysterical manifestations? Similar manifestations can be brought about by hypnosis."

This tendency has not yet been entirely overcome by psychology. It has split the mind up into many classifications—the conscious, and the subconscious, and the infraconscious, and the superconscious, and the co-conscious, and so on; not to mention the liminals. That is a correct enough procedure, for special purposes. But the trouble is that once this purely theoretical division is made there is an almost overmastering temptation to make it hard and fast. The mind is split into airtight compartments. Its divisions, and the subdivisions of the divisions, are too much treated as separate and individual things. One cannot see the woods for the trees.

Furthermore, having made these tight and separate compartments, there comes into being another strong temptation; and that is to use one or the other as a dump into which to thrust what we otherwise cannot explain. The "subconscious" is such a wastebasket. Anything that seems mysterious to anybody, from inexcusable tantrums to strange psychic adventure, may be referred to the "Subconscious" and comfortably forgotten for the time being. So common has been this habit—especially in the more popular writings on the subject—that the man on the street has accepted the word as a real explanation. That is due to the workings of the subconscious mind" is a phrase that has gained in his ears an accurate scientific value. Of course it is really no explanation at all.

Another, and related danger in psychological method is a tendency to build wide but fragmentary hypotheses on the basis of a small group of observed facts. The subject is so new, and the facts to be observed are so fascinating and suggestive, that theories spring up almost spontaneously. That is a commendable evidence of vitality and useful; provided one appreciates the situation. But unfortunately the zeal of the explorer in fresh and unknown land carries him away. He is apt to become preoccupied with the paramount importance of his theory, attempting to make it supreme where it should be only one piece in a pattern; observing his new facts only in reference to it; exacting his ingenuity in bending these facts to fit.

That is entirely natural. It is a concomitant of youth. When we examine historically the maturer sciences we find that they have gone through exactly the same stage. There must always exist a period of independent researchers, each busy with his own especial small bit of the subject. That bit must be, to him, the most important thing in life or he would not give his life to it. Furthermore, when he has observed enough facts, he is compelled by the nature of his mind to theorize about them. And since his vision is apt to be narrowed to the focus of what is under his microscope, to the exclusion of the general field, it is only natural that each should sense the general field in terms of his specialty.

This is not an indictment of psychology or its methods, nor is it anything more than a general warning to be used in some cases. Psychological theory has a great imaginative appeal. Furthermore, it is stimulating to the imagination. The student is likely to read into a hypothesis more than its author intended to put in. The man on the street is almost certain to seize on any fragment of provisional supposition and run off with it as a complete and workable whole. The Sunday supplements and "popular" treatises help him to that.

2

It is necessary to remember always that all these divisions of the mind are arbitrary. They are made as labels of classification, identifying tags for dissection. They are accurate in detail, but they purposely take little or no account of the universal principle of continuity, unity. They neglect to remind themselves—and us—that the mind is after all *one thing*.

In order to see that in its perspective, let us drop the thought of the mind for a moment and go back consciousness. Consciousness is the awareness of any entity. To become aware it must have an apparatus to function with; an awareness-mechanism. That we have been over before.

In what manner do you and I become aware? Obviously, first of all, by the physical sensation or response of our bodies. Next by our instinctive reactions, as most of the activities of the lower animals are governed. Then above that we are aware through the considered intellectual processes of our thoughts. But this does not complete the list. We recognize intuition as a definite awareness. It is akin to instinct, and by many it is confused with instinct; but it deals with a different and higher stimulus. Above that, and still more vaguely, we acknowledge what has been called direct inspiration. The latter two are the "things that come to us," without conscious intention of our intellects,—indeed often they work best when the intellect is entirely in abeyance.

These divisions are quite arbitrary, made for the purpose of discussion. From the point of view of consciousness they are all one thing—awareness. Nevertheless, they are recognizably defined, and are widely enough acknowledged to be each a subject of investigation by a different group of specialists. The first awareness-responses, those of the body, are studied by anatomists and physiologists; the second by naturalists; the third by the classic psychologists; the last two are just lately being rescued from the wastebasket of the "Subconscious" by modern psychology. They are all as diverse as can be. The methods by which they are observed and investigated are wide apart. *Nevertheless, they are all one thing.*

How can that be? We can best approach explanation through an analogy. Consider white light. Broken by a prism it shows us a series of different colors which we recognize instantly when we see them. We name them arbitrarily for the purposes of discussion—red, yellow, green, blue and violet. We recognize them plainly by sight, and also a number of their intermediates.

Nevertheless, science will inform us that from one end of the spectrum to the other there is an orderly and continuous progression without any divisions whatever. It is entirely a matter of wavelength, of speed of vibration. At the red end they are slower and longer, at the violet end they are faster and shorter. That is all. Furthermore, they increase and shorten in smooth arithmetical ratio. We should be hard put to it if we were required to name the precise rate at which blue ceases and purple begins, or to assign any difference in kind between the blue and the purple. They are the same thing, and the difference between is in degree, not in kind. There are no actual boundaries between any groups of constituents whatever, from one end to the other. The whole thing, taken together, undivided by the prism, we call one thing—white light.

The analogy is already apparent. The mind portion of our consciousness, which is our awareness, may also be considered to progress in orderly unbroken fashion from the red of physical sensation at one end to the ultraviolet of the highest inspiration at the other. Again it is not a difference of kind, but of degree. How we happen to be affected depends entirely on where we happen to be functioning. If that functioning is through the contacts and nerves of our physical bodies, our awareness response will be through sensation. If we are functioning through the back part of our brains, we will be utilizing our instinctive acquisitions; if through the front part we will respond by thought. If we are functioning through those higher powers we are only dimly beginning to understand, our awareness-responses are through the "unconscious,"—or the super-conscious, or the higher subconscious, or whatever we please to name it. Then we gain intuitions, or inspirations, But throughout *it is the same response in kind.* From one end of the scale to the other we are simply traversing one thing— what we might call the white light of consciousness. In all probability as finite beings we can never see it as white light. It must, to us, always be refracted through physical manifestations of one sort or another. Without such a manifestation we would go back beyond the markers to the Inunderstandable, the cosmic white light which has been variously named,—God, the Spirit, All-consciousness.

3

Evolution from this angle is a progression along this rainbow path. Some creations live in pure physical sensation; others have physical sensation *plus* instinct; still others have attained to thought. Whether there are any created beings anywhere who can center their beings in what are still to us intuitive or inspirational perceptions, I do not know. The creature is centered, focused so to speak, on that point of selection where its state of development enables it to dwell to the best advantage. It is the restricting point, the place where, from the millions of stimuli constantly offering, the few that can be used are appropriated and the rest screened off. Like any focusing point things there are clear but limited: things outside are more or less blurred.

Such a focusing point is extremely necessary. We are already very complex creatures. Things by the myriad beat upon us. Were it not for the guardian at the portal we should live in a bewilderment. Our physical senses are daily receiving and dutifully reporting instantly and completely literally millions of impressions to our center of consciousness.

Dr. Jackson, in a book called *Outwitting Our Nerves*, expresses this vividly:

> Only by a certain degree of irritability can it survive in the struggle for existence. The five senses are simply different phases of the apparatus for receiving communications from the outside world. Other parts of the machinery catch the manifold messages pouring into the brain from within our bodies themselves.
>
> These communications cannot be stopped, nor can we prevent their impress on the cells of the brain or the spinal cord, but we do have a good deal to say as to which ones shall be brought into the

focus of attention and receive enough notice to become real, conscious sensations. If a human being had to give conscious attention to every stimulus from the outer world and from his own body to every signal which flashes itself along his sensory nerves to his brain, he would need a different kind of mind from his present efficient but limited apparatus. ... The stream of consciousness never stops, not even in sleep. ...

During any five minutes of a walk down a city street a man has hundreds of visual images flashed upon the retina of the eye. His eye sees every little line in the faces of the passers-by, every detail of their clothing, the decorations on the buildings, the street signs overhead, the articles in the shop windows, the paving of the sidewalks, the curbing and the tracks which he crosses, and scores of other objects to most of which the man himself is oblivious. His ear hears every sound within hearing distance,—the honk of every horn, the clang of every bell, the voices of people and the shuffle of feet. Some part of his mind feels the press of his foot on the pavement, the rubbing of his heel on his stocking, the touch of his clothing all over his body, and all of those so-called kinesthetic sensations,—sensations of motion and balance which keep him in equilibrium and on the move, to say nothing of the never-ending stream of messages from every cell of every muscle and tissue of his body.

The subconscious mind knows and needs to know, what is happening in the farthermost cell of the body.

It needs to know at any moment where the knees are, and the feet; otherwise the individual would fall in a heap whenever he forgot to watch his step. It needs to know just how much light is entering the eye, and how much blood is in the stomach. ... Its messages never cease.

This is on the physical side only. In addition are what must be an equal or greater volume of psychic impressions beating upon the individual.

If we were to be intellectually aware of them all, we would be helpless. But just as we are saved from confusing intellectual awareness of our bodily perception by the fact that our particular mechanism is focused more or less accurately to our particular need, so we cannot doubt that the same thing obtains as to other awareness-mechanisms than those of our senses; that we are focused on our need from all the unguessed influences of cosmos, millions of impressions that impact upon our instinctive and intuitional and Inspirational faculties. Were all these to obtain equal recognition our powers of assimilation would be overpassed. The focusing is the selecting device.

We might then define, very broadly, the intellect of any creature as its points of focus on the spectrum. We are here considering intellect not necessarily as a reasoning faculty, capable of creative thought; but as that center from which the creature's present activities are directed. If that seems unduly to expand the word intellect, some other word may be substituted.

Now it is very evident that, considering the spectrum of consciousness as a whole, and not merely as an individual possession, this focusing point may rest at different places for different creatures, or at different places for the same creature at different times. What is above the focusing point to A must appear to him as intuitive or inspirational, and somewhat vague. Out of focus, in other words. But B, more highly developed, might focus farther along. In that case B's point of intellect— the center from which he makes his selections—would be in what to A is still the intuitive region. And further, as either goes on to development, each tends to enter into what *has* been heretofore his superconscious and to appropriate more and more of its powers and responses in his actively selecting mechanism.

In the imperfectly examined but stupendous possibilities of the "subconscious" that psychology is just beginning to show us, we may vaguely foreshadow powers that may one day be included within the focusing point of our conscious control. And herein we see the horizon of infinite development.

CHAPTER 17

THE EXTENDED MEMORY

~

1

HOWEVER that may be for the future, the fact is that at present we are each individually concerned with his own progress. This takes place through experience and memory. But among all the things that happen to us there are certain vital experiences that make the most for progress, and which we remember. They become more intimately part of our individual content. These are the ones in which we have used our volition, made our choice, exercised our free will.[1] Every such experience is through this mechanism drawn from that part of the cosmos which comprises the Not-done, and transferred

---

[1] Some might question this, asking, how about the passive bystander or subject of an experience? Though having nothing active to do with the experience, he would remember it. But has not the free will had its share in such cases? The personal interpretation is often a direct act of free will. And that personal interpretation would be utterly impossible were it not for a long series of other experiences in the past by which the bias and character and equipment—in short, the receptivity—of the spectator was established. And these were the result of free will. We must never lose sight of the fact that no act, mental or spiritual or physical, can stand alone. It is the descendant in direct lineage of a long and unbroken series. For observe, two such "passive spectators" of the same thing will get from it two entirely different reactions, two totally distinct influences, two widely divergent experiences,—and hence memories. This was not because at the moment of this particular happening they differently applied the free will; but because in innumerable instances in the past, in a myriad of different but contributing experiences, each has differently used his power.

to that part of the cosmos which comprises the Thing-done. It has been accomplished because we personally were aware of it, and made a choice. Therefore, it must have become part of our individual memory, and cannot be lost. It is our possession. For some reason or another we may not be able at will to place our hands on any particular one of these possessions; nevertheless they are there, and can, by a proper assembly of conditions, be brought intact to the conscious mind.

Experience without the assistance of free will brings development, as we have seen. But what we have also seen, without having noticed it, is that an act in which free will is involved brings a *double* experience. That is so because a choice is involved. The person must know two things before choice is possible; whereas a creature that merely reacts needs know only the stimulus that causes the reaction. The former knows what it has chosen to do, of course; but it also knows what it has chosen not to do. When one picks up a grain of sand, he does not take all the other grains of sand. Thus the exercise of free will, through the fact that it doubles experience, is imperative for the fullest and the fastest development. If one would construct for himself a course of conduct, he must keep this point to the forefront.

We must here remind ourselves that exercise of the real free will is not so frequent as it seems to be. Of course the word "will" is not intended here to borrow anything from the strenuous upwards and onwards who clamor for the development of "will power," meaning merely a tense and generally futile concentration, as far as real results go.

This also should be noted: that with the first exercise of the free will a creature comes into some sort of intended relation with the whole of cosmos. As we have just pointed out, he knows the thing he has chosen; and in a more or less vague way all the things he has not chosen. He has differentiated them, consciously; and he has taken an attitude toward each group. For the first time he has come out of limited automatic contact, and into at least potential cosmic contact. His relation with the not-chosen component is very nebulous, of course. *It is, like all other beginnings,* a germ. But he has ceased to be a mere thing, and has become a citizen of the world.

And in so doing for the first time he is occupied, as far as he is concerned, primarily in building up *himself,* and only secondarily in building up the quality of consciousness from which he has sprung.

2

Here begins, then, still another responsibility; that as respects himself. Just to the extent that his fate is in his own hands, and to no further extent, is he responsible for his own individuality. He is not merely subjected to development; he has an obligation of development. He must give his mind to the job. You remember the essence of that job;—"to practice, with all the equipment he possesses, in being Me."

To do this he must possess, or build, or evolve slowly some system of conduct. This system of conduct we call ethics. It has many branches. In its deeper aspects it is not a set of rules, but a spiritual hygiene.

3

That term has a thousand facets. On one side it Comprises at once a development of powers, an exercise of powers, and a command of powers. As far as our command of the particular faculty we have lately been discussing is concerned—memory—that, as we know in our own cases, is capable of cultivation and extension. The simplest of the advertised memory systems can do wonders. One can practice and remember at sight Jack Robinson and where one met him ten years ago and that he had trouble with his wife and his teeth. Also telephone numbers by the gross, and dates in history, and statistics of the cotton crop in 1894, and to do all one's errands without the aid of a notebook, and many other curious and more or less useful or useless things. One can also be taught how to cultivate the ability to recollect, to find and open dockets of the past that otherwise would have been filed away in dusty desuetude. Many of these locked cabinets may be entered by one means or another—by progressive training, by the "free association" of the psychoanalysts, by hypnotism—and their contents brought to conscious attention. It is by no means a wild dream to prognosticate that in some remote time man will obtain access to and command of all this material he so industriously accumulates, and buries, and preserves. We are already, feebly, learning methods by which a small percentage of such a result may be brought about.

But beyond this, there seems to be no logical reason why man's command over the other type of memory—that peculiar not merely to himself, but to the whole quality of consciousness—may not also be extended. The body of it is there; and the connection is by the nature of things established, albeit vaguely. Intuition, inspiration, lucidity are as yet uncertain, freakish, out of control. Instances such as that of my friend in Switzerland may be fairly classed—as far as we can see—as accidental. Nevertheless, the beginnings of some little control have been made. We have as yet no clear vision of how these beginnings are correlated; indeed in most cases they seem to have little connection one with the other. Hypnotism is one little hand-hold: likewise certain aspects of certain kinds of trance; there are a few artists in one medium or another, who certainly work from inspiration, who can to an extent command that inspiration. And soon. It appears to be reason--able that this simple germ too will grow.

At the present time we can have little to say as to means and methods. It does seem, however, that command of the quality memory must depend on the degree to which one's contact-possibilities are developed toward race consciousness rather than merely personal consciousness. The wider one's human sympathies, the more power does one attain. That statement has long been a commonplace of figurative speech. Here it is taken from the figurative and placed solidly in the practical.

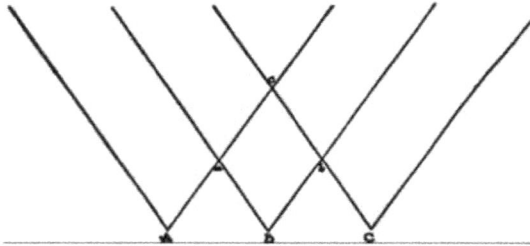

Perhaps this can be better illustrated by the graph.

A, B and C are individuals, and these letters also represent the beginnings of individual experiences for each. At point *a* the body of experience or memory of A and B overlap and become common to both, though A and C are still separate and apart. At point *b* the experiences of B and C coincide. At point *c*, however, if the expansion continues, the areas of all three overlap, and so there exists something common to all. Instead of A, B and C substitute the individuals of the race. It is evident that,—provided expansion takes place—it does not matter how far apart are the inceptions; there must come a time—if evolution continues—when experience and memory must overlap. Carried far enough, it would theoretically become racial.

This is an illustration merely. The point is that with increasing development each individual must possess in his own consciousness—though perhaps as yet deeply hidden and inaccessible to his volition—not only the personal experiences and memories on which he has exercised his own free will, but also many others. These, to repeat, are accessible to him only in a limited way. They come to his conscious attention only rarely, and apparently by accident. But he must possess a portion of the experience and memory of, at first smaller, and later larger groups. In perfection he would possess that of his whole quality of consciousness. By development and expansion they become part of his possessions as much as though his own free will had manufactured them. He should have to them the same access as to those he might naturally consider his own. In the expansion toward wider inclusion, and in the discovery and perfection of the technique of handling his possessions, lie one of man's greatest possibilities of growth.

4

This is of course a far cast into what must be a remote future. It has value to us now as furnishing one building stone for the structure of our spiritual hygiene, when we come to its construction. In our present state of enlightenment this sort of acquisition must take place, if at all, in the farther region of the mind over which man's control is little or nil. But in order intelligently to move, we must establish direction.

CHAPTER 18

CONSCIOUSNESS IS

~

1

OUTSIDE our conditions of space and time, We must again and again remind ourselves, is an Absolute which we cannot understand. We may come into relation with it, and we may attempt to analyze that relationship from our own point of view; we may find it to be, in some manner personal to ourselves, in touch with our individual aspirations and in response to our individual needs. That is a matter that each must determine for himself. The relations one finds to be true in his own case may well be one of intimacy, of close knit correspondence—the loving God. This is all understandable and possible. For the one thing we can predicate concerning so ungraspable a thing as the infinite is that all things are possible to it. Otherwise it would not be the infinite.

But we must with all this keep clearly before our minds that the infinite cosmos is inunderstandable by anything but itself. In our approach toward it we must be satisfied with momentary, half-guessed glimpses, as we see mountain tops through shifting clouds. And we must remember that in discussion of higher truth no man can be told anything that he does not already know. The idea, the form-of-words, must find within him a thing that has grown through his own spiritual development of perception. This he must already be possessed of inside, in order that the idea expressed from the outside may find its correspondence. Otherwise, any statement is a mere collection of words, with perhaps a beguiling surface meaning.

Indeed this is a profound truth that applies to all interchange. In the realm of abstract truth man can tell another man nothing that he does not already know. The latter may not know that he knows it, but he must have grown to its essence before he can understand more than the surface significance of what the other is talking about.

One can start another in the direction of acquisition; one can bring to the surface what has remained submerged, formulate what has been obscure; that is all.

It is also a twin-sister truth, or perhaps merely another way of saying the same truth,—that we are capable of understanding only that to whose dimensions we have grown. It is possible to feel intuitively, momentarily, something beyond that, of course; but when we attempt to give it a shape and form, that shape and form will be molded to the dimensions of our greatest capacity as determined by the growth we have made. That is why any attempt at concrete expression of God by man is in man's own image. The expression may, in the case of the modern philosopher, no longer be anthropomorphic;[1] but it is nevertheless an expression in terms of his own highest possibilities as he can conceive them. That is all that a sincere effort at concrete expression of God, in any state of civilization, can be—an embodiment of the highest conception of himself possible to man in that state of civilization.

This is on the side of intellect, of formulation, of an attempt to get a definite conception of something before which to bow. On the side of feeling, of spiritual contact, communion, mysticism—whatever one pleases to call it—wherein is no attempt at intellectual conception, the relation may be as close, as intimate, as beautiful as each one's capacity permits.

Nevertheless, there are a few intellectual ideas, of the greatest simplicity, which we can permit ourselves. This Consciousness is. There are very few wholly mechanistic philosophers or scientists who feel they have reached any finality of view. Those who avow such a belief, do so tentatively. "We do not see—as yet—how it can be otherwise," is the gist of their statement of position. The whole trend and effort of such men's investigations show them to be still on their journey, still focused, still blindered for a purpose, still on the arc of the incomplete circle. They are immersed in detail, following short trails. Their generalizations are

---

[1] In the immediate literal sense—God in man's physical image.

as yet only generalizations into what are really larger details. For it is an interesting and significant fact that the greater scientists who have lived out the essential completion of their investigations and theories have returned at last, and have in most cases testified to, a conviction of the animating absolute Consciousness. These men have in most cases stepped aside in order to make a formal statement to the end that it should be clearly understood that over and above and beyond the intricate detail of method with which their scientific lives had been concerned, they have entertained a profound faith. Darwin, Newton, Spencer, Huxley, Lodge,—the list could be far extended,—have taken the pains to make a plain affirmation of this faith. Even La Place, whose life work apparently was the coveting of the visible universe to a self-acting mechanism, considered it necessary to make such a statement. No one could deny the thoroughness of these men's scientific insight; nor the rigidity of their scientific method. But each had, as far as himself was concerned, and in the essentials, completed his allotted task; each had successfully traversed the thicket of facts; each was permitted to look back for a survey of the whole. Only those still threading the tangled paths have been unable to see the wood for the trees, to realize that there must be something beyond the mechanism, perfect though that mechanism may be.

To most of us who are at all open to influences outside ourselves the conviction that this Consciousness *is* comes to us almost in spite of ourselves. We must be aware at least of some vast and beautiful life-giving force that continually expresses itself all around us. We see it everywhere: the busy clouds, the drawing power of the sun, the new shoots in our garden; everywhere the urge and developing growing power of life. Thousands of us have spent our thousands of years in research and observation, and we have not yet been able even to catalogue a thousandth part of the things that surround us. We have not succeeded in understanding more than a little of their beautiful interplays and interrelations and interdependencies. Everywhere we turn our intelligence we see, by its own test, that things are intelligently arranged. And we must, if we are at all sensitive or imaginative, see that we ourselves are part of that system; that we too are animated by that same urging and life giving force; that we float in it so to speak, and are part of it as it is part of us, and that from it we draw at least our power of existence.

That much we can know. And we know that this universal life giving force answers need when approached in harmony with itself. Some people see further in this direction than do others. But in the very simplest aspect of this we say that we "work with nature." We cannot by our own strength lift the sawlog and move it to the water; but we can call to our aid the forces of gravity and it slips to the sea. We have felt and expressed a need, and there is in the mechanism of the universe a definite answer to that need. But the answer is available only when we invoke it by an act of volition. We cannot sit supine and expect our sawlog to be transported for us. That is not the way of nature.

This is on the purely mechanical and material side. Nevertheless, the response to need is here no different in kind than that which meets the mystic's outreaching. Nor is it different from the response that meets the need when an emergency taps in us an unsuspected clarity of vision, readiness of expedient, resourcefulness, and strength beyond our normal powers. It is all a part of the universal life in which, to repeat, we float and from which we draw our power of existence. The complement to ourselves exists, and requires only the proper evocation. Our education consists precisely in the method of this proper evocation: it will always so consist, in higher and higher medium of expression.

2

Only vaguely or here and there have men realized fully in this field what has long been known to obtain in others:—that the obscure methods of the higher branches may to advantage be studied in the more simple and perhaps crude methods of the lower. If we would construct for ourselves a spiritual hygiene we can perhaps get more than a hint in the ordinarily physical things we do every day. And then try them out to see if they will work. As Dooley says, 'Av it worruks it's true."

It is not the purpose at present to attempt the construction of even a simple spiritual hygiene. Perhaps in some future work I may make the attempt. But an example of what we are here discussing may be found in a study of the technique of any accurate game—golf, pistol shooting, tennis, archery. The first thing that the beginner discovers, and the last thing he acquires practically, is that physical tension is fatal to good results. One must be free-moving, relaxed. Concentration in the sense of tightness and a convoluted self-contained effort defeats its own aim, It does so for the simple reason that he throws himself entirely on his own self-contained resources. He is working by personal intellectual effort, outside the rhythm of nature. The result is awkwardness. All he learns is the ease with which his strength is overpassed. And as we ascend in the scale we will find that the same consideration obtains: that receptivity, porosity, permeability—whatever one pleases to call it,—gives access to that unknown reservoir that manifests itself in body or mind or spirit as more than normal endurance or resourcefulness or inspiration; while tension, self-centeredness, hard compactness of soul results at best in awkwardness and at worst in retrogression. That knowledge is coming to us slowly, and piecemeal, and in many different ways. We are gaining control of the powers we know; and we are becoming increasingly aware of powers yet to come.

3

This intimate relationship between ourselves, as consciousness, and the Consciousness of which we—and all other things,—are manifestations, must exist not merely in one but in every aspect of our beings. The thing is homogeneous. There is no reason why it should be otherwise. In Consciousness as a whole is the complement to every need of any of its parts, could that complement be evoked.

Furthermore, Consciousness as a whole must be self-aware to an extent of which our own self-awareness is but a feeble and flickering shadow. It must be so. We cannot attempt to fathom its infinite aspects; but in the finite it possesses as awareness-mechanisms all created things. Through their evolution and development it has perfected its qualities. Through their physical manifestations as sense organs—so to speak—it has the experience and memory of a universe.

It cannot be too often repeated that it is impossible for us to understand either the purpose, the nature, or the function of the Absolute. But we are entirely privileged to examine it in any of its finite aspects. We are conditioned in our thoughts and activities by space and time; and in so far as the Absolute also conditions itself in space and time it is within our ken. With that limitation, as we are constituted, we are potentially capable of understanding. Nothing within our limit markers is finally unknowable. We are justified in pushing our inquiries out and out, as far as our vision extends, confident that nothing within our view is intrinsically inunderstandable, however mysterious or "holy" it may for the moment appear. And slowly but steadily we are extending our comprehension out into the "'unknowable." To the savage the movements of the stars, the reactions of the bodily functions, the source of the thunderbolt are alike "unknowable." Often, they were held sacred. As finite creatures we are heirs to all of the finite. And whatever aspect the Absolute therein presents is a legitimate field of investigation.

The ultimate purpose is beyond us, because it is infinite. Why the Absolute conditions itself in space and time is and must remain obscure. But *so conditioned* its purpose seems to be plain. It is that of each and every one of its creatures:—*the expansion of self-consciousness by increasing awareness.*

4

As we have several times speculated, from as many different angles, this increasing awareness seems to be gained through the awareness-mechanisms of its own manifestations and embodiments. We now begin to see in what manner it is in relation to those embodiments, and why the meed of healing wisdom or urge or complement answers need.

An illustrative picture may be constructed from the analogy of the human body. The governing center of the human being has care of the health of its body. By governing center I do not mean the conscious intellect so much as that aspect of the ego which carries on the mechanical processes—digestion, circulation, the beating of the heart, the intaking of the breath, the reflexes of the nerves, the dispatch of hormones—in short, all the intricate body politic of the physical functions. This is a definite and very complex intelligence, working with a marvelous executive capacity. If something happens, if an injury is inflicted, or a disintegration of tissue takes place, this intelligence takes cognizance and at once sets about the proper measures for relief. It hurries up its armies of combat, its agents of reconstruction. The invaded territory entertains for the emergency a whole military population of quite different character from its usual inhabitants. If the campaign is successful, the combat troops are withdrawn; after the scavengers have thrown out the debris, they too retire; and the field is restored to the peaceful occasions of its normal population.

This executive intelligence is in the main below our threshold. However, it has in some cases been slightly raised to a more or less conscious but always partial control. Our various excursions into auto-suggestion, mental healing, Coué-ism, miracle cures and the like have given us at least a hint of the extent of this executive supervision.

For a long time we have emphasized the idea that healthy cells made a healthy person. We are beginning to see that in fact the thing is reciprocal; that the person himself can contribute toward the healthy cells. The central consciousness sends aid when it is needed.

But we note this: that these reparatory forces are marshalled and sent by the central consciousness to an affected part only when the central consciousness is informed of the trouble. The mind[2] instructs the hand to pull away from the candle flame because the finger has reported, through pain, that its tissue is being destroyed, and clamors for the assistance of a command to the muscles of the arm. If we should numb the nerves, or sever them, the finger would char unknown. That is a simple illustration, on the side of usually voluntary action, but it is typical. In order to extend its help, in order to complement the need, the central being must be apprised through an appropriate mechanism.

In an analogous manner we can conceive consciousness flooding toward the need of any of its creatures the influences most healing of disharmony of any kind. In a not dissimilar fashion we might conceive of the necessity for its being apprised of that need, at least in the case of those creatures to whom we might ascribe an enduring individuality. And when it is not so apprised—when that particular mechanism which is the nerve-system of the complicated awareness creature not touched—the soul may char unknown.

The mechanism of appraisal has been variously defined in different ages and by different schools of thought. Many of the definitions have been outworn, or have gathered to themselves superfluous and undesirable connotations. Some have become obsolete; some are almost ready for the discard; some are even now in the process of formulation. It has been called prayer; but that word has become almost too tainted with theological formalism, and its intellectual aspect has overshadowed its essence of subjectivity. It might be called spiritual openness, relaxation, communion, porosity, permeability, spiritual contact. Whatever the term, itself must be understood and used as the cornerstone of any spiritual hygiene. And in the case of those creatures endowed with free will, it must be sought. One "works with nature" by choice. It is another of the functions and privileges and responsibilities of free will. The simpler creatures obtain what they need automatically. The current of consciousness flows through them unimpeded, and they take from it their requirements as the variegated cells of the body take from the passing blood stream their own especial constituents. But here the power passes more into individual control.

---

[2] Perhaps only the instinctive aspect of the mind.

It is as though one possessed a switch by which he turned the current of his need into contact with the greater consciousness of which he is part, or by which he cut himself off.

Needless to say this conception must not be narrowed to the sort of personal attention the ancient Jews thought they obtained from their diminishment of God,—Jehovah. It is a turning of health-giving currents of all that is required of all that Consciousness contains towards a needing part. If the being is open and receptive, it flows within him and accomplishes. If he is tight in his tension of impermeability, it washes by him and but a little trickle enters in.

But beware again of an attempt at full understanding of Consciousness. You will merely be constructing a gigantic man to fill all space.

CHAPTER 19

I AM

~

1

WE have repeated a number of times and in a number of different ways the thought that in essential the universe represents the finite aspect of the universal life or force or vitality or consciousness seeking through development to become self-aware. We have also been made familiar with the method of this becoming. It is in process exactly the same method by which any entity becomes self-aware;—by knowing something outside its center.

This presupposes a duality, but it is a finite duality in infinite unity. It exists only within the limit markers we have set for ourselves; but it exists throughout all the space included between them. In the very first juxtaposition of the two specks of consciousness, of the electron and proton, we find that out of the same thing two things have come: a force and something representing that force. Whatever its infinite aspect, within the finite the All-Consciousness realizes its I AM, just as do any of its specialized manifestations; by awareness of itself. This awareness,—again like that of its creatures—comes through response contacts. These response contacts make experience and memory: their increasing numbers and complexity, as evolution proceeds, make for that growth toward perfect self-awareness which—as far as we can see—appears to be the ultimate purpose within the finite.

Now we have further noted the evident fact that in order to get awareness-contacts, it is necessary to possess awareness-mechanisms. That, also, is true of everything. On the physical side, the gills of the fish and the lungs of the air-breathing creatures are at once mechanisms of life and of response to individual necessity and environment. The various faculties of body, mind and spirit are all awareness-mechanisms.

The awareness-mechanisms of Consciousness within the finite are its created beings. Each represents to a greater or lesser degree of perfection according to its development some quality or idea of consciousness; it makes consciousness self-aware as to its own particular self. The different ideas, or qualities, are worked out little by little through their repeated embodiment, and by means of the increasing self-awareness such embodiment makes possible.

All this is old ground. It is repeated here in condensed form in order that we may again have the principle clearly in mind.

But what we have not particularly considered before is that though all created things are separate one from the other, and are quite distinct entities, nevertheless they are all informed by, animated by the one thing. Traced back in pedigree, through whatever intricate device, they become at last components of Consciousness as a whole. They are as distinct and as individual as the different corpuscles of the blood; but they are as much a part of the universal life as the corpuscles are part of our own vitality. Looked upon as physical bodies they are mere filters of life. It flows through them; they are immersed in it, suspended in it. It is like a surrounding atmosphere, all embracing, all inclusive, containing in itself all elements of all things. Each entity can take of these elements what its need requires and what its equipment permits. All that is necessary is that it remain permeable. To maintain permeability is, again, a portion of the spiritual hygiene. There is, in this conception, no merging of individualities. They are distinct because each is an organ of awareness. Each is as much an organ of self-awareness as is the eye or the ear to the human being; and as specialized. We would never confuse our ears and our eyes. Each has its own function. Each is aiding, in its own way, through its own bit of self-awareness, the Consciousness in the finite to become self-aware.

This is all abstractly metaphysical. It begins to strike home when we narrow the field and look upon ourselves. We, too, are awareness-mechanisms of the finite Consciousness.

From our own point of view, at least, we are an exceedingly delicate and responsive instrument, of constantly increasing efficiency. We are able to become aware of ourselves in a great many ways. Compared with the simple physical correspondences of the fish, our bodies, with their beautiful balanced sensitiveness, are of much higher value. We can see color in shade and arrangement, and form, and delicacy beyond the capacity of any other animal. We can see more things, and larger things, and smaller things in a greater variety of relations. There are some specialists—like eagles and buzzards—that can beat us in certain small departments of the game, but we can beat them in so many others that our superiority can hardly be questioned. No eagle could make anything out of a painting nor match a ribbon. Training of intellect? Certainly: but through the eyes. We are visually more aware. Similarly we can hear more, and taste more, and even smell more, in the sense of becoming more deeply aware of things, than other organisms. On the intellectual, the correlating, side we are, of course, miles beyond. The most complicated intellectual synthesis possible to an animal is easy for the most undeveloped savage. All this is awareness. As organs of awareness we may flatter ourselves that we are fairly sensitive and responsive. In the universe *as we know it* we represent some senses that are apparently not duplicated elsewhere. Through us the finite Consciousness becomes aware in directions it could not be aware had we not been developed. Just as a man cannot see if deprived of his eyes.

Each of the bodily sense organs has its specialty to which it attends, and which cannot be taken care of by any other organ. The eye is responsible for the responses possible to light vibrations; the ear to those of sound; touch to pressure contacts, and so on. In a similar manner we, as awareness organs, may be conceived to have our specialties, so to speak. Consciousness through us becomes aware more fully of certain things. One of those things seems to be the free will. We are, as far as our own vision extends, the best mechanism through which the finite Consciousness becomes aware of itself on the side of free will.

2

Accepting this view, even speculatively, the implications are enormous. It goes far to explain the existence of what we call evil; but which might more accurately be defined as disharmony.

Disharmony is a state of unbalance, of lack of equilibrium, and hence of discomfort. Discomfort, in its broadest sense, extends so far as to include suffering of all sorts.

For we must conceive that self-awareness on the side of free will is as yet far from complete. It is, like all faculties, like all creatures, like all ideas, in the process of perfection through the usual methods of trial and error; of experiment, abandoned or modified for re-use. It gropes. It struggles toward a more and more perfect, a more and more complete manifestation and understanding of itself. It must learn by its failures and half successes how to handle itself.

In the construction of the human body the eye is the mechanism by which one becomes aware of the form and color of his surroundings. Without the eye one would know little or nothing of these things. But suppose that some constructing Intelligence, having made the eye with this end and capacity, had gone farther and given it the power to decide for itself what it would or would not pass through its lenses to be reported to the brain, and in what form! Until the eye had found by its own experience that it did not pay to report a level plain where a precipice yawned, or an open prospect instead of the forest of brambles simply because plains and open prospects pleased it while precipices and brambles did not, there would be trouble. Trouble for the owner of the eye, and therefore for the eye itself. For the health and well-being of the lesser depends on the whole. Only when by repeated experiment had it dawned on the eye that harmony and cooperation meant health and happiness would its owner become completely aware of reality and not of delusion. And it is probable that it would also dawn on the eye that it was possessed of some responsibility!—The fundamental responsibility of those creatures endowed with free will is not too unlike that crude illustration. For it is through themselves, as awareness-mechanisms, that the All-conscious is becoming more fully aware of one aspect of its finite self.

This type of responsibility is another ingredient that must be taken into account when we come to the construction, each for himself, of a spiritual hygiene in accordance with which to live. For though no human being can look into the greater Consciousness with other understanding than he brings to the contemplation of his own, it would not be too far a cry to guess that when its aware-ness-response, through its creatures of free will, is of harmony with the basic law, it experiences pleasure as we experience pleasure in like case. And that when those mechanisms respond to disharmony, it feels the pain which our own personal disharmony—of body for example—brings to us. And that the struggle toward self-awareness, through mistake, through ignorance, through the slow obstruction of disharmony, the feeling of effort, of triumph in achievement or of temporary defeat, as reported or reflected or embodied in the countless multitudes of its creatures, is not unlike in kind our gropings upward.

CHAPTER 20

THE CLOCKMAKER'S ILLUSION

~

1

WE have skirted many times in the preceding pages a most fascinating subject for speculation. It is one which we must examine to some extent, if only for the purpose of determining how much may lie within our deliberately set limit markers. I refer to space and time.

It is no part of my intention to go into anything purporting to be an exhaustive discussion. Anyone interested may in the nearest good library go as far as he likes, even into the elusive abstractions of the fourth dimension, or the equally elusive speculations of the Einstein school as to three dimensioned space. The fourth dimension may be something into which eventually we shall grow, but it does not seem at present to be one of our immediately determining conditions.[1] When we occupy ourselves with our present position and conduct we deal with three dimensioned space only. The reasoning I am about to undertake, and the conclusions I shall draw, will be considered by the deeper student as fragmentary and more or less elementary. But my

---

[1] Anyone interested in getting at as clear a conception of what is meant by the fourth dimension as is possible to a beginner would better read Ouspensky's *Tertium Organum*: then try Hinton.

intention is to consider only those aspects of the subject which are necessary foundation stones to whatever solid belief each may eventually wish to construct.

2

What is this space and time by which we are conditioned? In the primitive view that question seems to be as simple as the one which asked for a distinction between living things and non-living things. But pressed home the inquiry is elusive. Even the primitive realizes that as far as we ourselves are concerned there is nothing positive about either. An hour to a lover is not at all the same thing as an hour to a prisoner: a mile to the motorist is quite different from the mile of the fellow afoot carrying a heavy pack and with a sprained ankle. We counter this thought by saying that the thing should not be considered subjectively. There are definite standards, the same for everybody. Clocks will measure the hour; and a yardstick will measure the mile.

That sounds reasonable. Whence the clock? and who decided on the yardstick? That, of course, is easy. The clock's hour is determined by the speed of revolution of our globe; and the yard is a definite fraction of the globe's diameter.[2] It does not matter whether one is a lover or a prisoner; a passenger or a pedestrian: an hour is an hour, and a mile is a mile.

We will accept that, for the moment, as far as we are concerned. But suppose for argument's sake there is intelligent life on Neptune, our most distant planet. Its year is 165 of our years; its diameter is over four times that of our earth. Even were they cognizant of our standards of measurement how much attention would the inhabitants of that planet pay to them, either subjectively or objectively? They would indubitably have their own hour, their own yardstick, which would be different from our own. Or let us examine any pebble under a powerful microscope. We will find ourselves looking from above on a rugged granite mountain. Perhaps under our immediate vision is a deep canyon, reaching down into unguessed depths, with dizzy cliffs and sheer breath-taking plunges into space. Never in all our travels have we peered into such an abyss. Even without imagining inhabitants for such an actually commodious world, how can we ourselves measure that space? Are we to conclude

---

[2] Not in origin. But the standard yard is now defined in terms of a meter, and a meter is based on the size of the earth.

that all intelligent individual consciousness in the universe exists on globes just the size of ours and with exactly its speed of rotation? The assumption borders on absurdity.

And where can we stop—in either direction? We have passed that pebble world a thousand times, and we and it mutually unconscious of each other: and on its tiny surface are other grains which a super-microscope—beyond our mechanical powers—could be conceived to expand to other complete landscapes of a wide spaciousness. There is room for many such expansions down to the millions of magnification which would make the molecule a globe the size of our own. Or imagine some greater entity looking down his microscope on our Grand Cañon; and he and our pebble of earth mutually unconscious of each other. And raise that scale again to an incomprehensible magnitude at which we can only guess. What then? How can we measure space by yardsticks? low are we even to give anything so elastic and changing a determinate and specific name?

3

Does it not become here almost self-evident that the only possible general standard of measurement cannot be anything but *degree of consciousness*. If we are to evaluate space at all it must be through the thing that is conditioned by it. To measure it we must take the point of view, so to speak, of the thing that is so conditioned. We must become for the purpose pebble-size, or us-size, or Neptune-size, or whatever.

This is an important thought. It seems, as I have said, fairly self-evident, but it must be seriously considered and absorbed, for it leads to another thought that is significant. It is this:

Since the above is true, it follows that space itself is an attribute of consciousness.

Do not get the idea that this means that space is an illusion, that it is a "figment of the imagination." It is as real as any other manifestation. But it is, like these other manifestations, an externalizing, so to speak, of Consciousness. It is, to repeat, one of its many attributes. And just as it is an attribute of Consciousness in general so we find—as we should expect—that in the microcosmos of ourselves it is also an attribute of our own individual consciousness. However rigid our yardstick may be, the basic fact remains that space is to each one of us a different thing. A thousand of those very uniform yards is one matter to a rifleman, another to a bowman. A mile is one thing to the savage and something quite different to the habitual motorist, and something still different to the cowboy. When we try to rigidify space by standards, we shall find this always to be the case. It must be one of the attributes of consciousness: it is content—what the individual is capable of perceiving. At the last we come to see that what we call distance is not space at all. Degrees of perception is space.

4

When we turn to the contemplation of time, we find that exactly the same considerations hold true. Indeed, from a deeply philosophic point of view—with which we will not meddle now,—time is considered in one of its more abstruse aspects as merely part of the fourth dimension of space. But it is not necessary to delve into those abstractions. In our own experience we will instantly acknowledge that in spite of the clock one minute may be quite unlike another. Again we need only remind ourselves that the prisoner's hour and the lover's hour have little kinship.

It is when in imagination we step outside our own degree of consciousness, however, that we see this most clearly. Again let us look down the barrel of our microscope wherein we discovered our vast worlds of a new space, but this time upon a drop of ditch water. We will see innumerable creatures darting here and there among the seas, bays, and estuaries of an intricate series of waterways. If we are sufficiently patient and enthusiastic, and had we some means of keeping track of a specific individual from among the swarming multitudes, we might follow one of these tiny organisms from birth to death without losing an inordinate amount of our valuable time. His whole voyage of life among the bays and estuaries and channels and open seas is compassed and finished while we look: and perhaps his whole teeming complicated world evaporates under our eyes. What impresses us about the whole thing is the extraordinary, the feverish speed of the whole process, the headlong dash of the tiny creatures.

We see one of them set sail from his harbor and speed across a channel to an opposite port. There he lingers for a fraction of a second, only to dart up a waterway and out beyond the field of vision. We estimate that his voyage took about a second, perhaps two.

How do we know? We have no authority for saying that, except as it affects our own particular degree of consciousness. As far as he is concerned, he may not be a hasty creature at all; but one of extreme and cautious deliberation. There is no earthly reason to suppose that his day-cycles take their regulation from our own days. Indeed, it is quite probable that what we might call his days—his alterations of rest and activity—are conditioned on quite other circumstances. While we watched him, in that two seconds accorded him, he may quite well have been coaling up in the first harbor several of his days. His voyage across the inlet may have been long and rather monotonous. In the second harbor he may have lingered in recuperation for a day or so more; and then started out, like Christopher Columbus, over vast and uncharted seas.

Or resume our hypothetical habitancy of Neptune. Is it quite likely that a Neptunite would experience the impression of waiting the duration of 165 years for spring to come around again? or would not the span of his year, in all probability, seem much the same to him as our year seems to us?

And so, when we come to evaluate time as we attempted to evaluate space, we are driven again to define it as an attribute of consciousness. In order to build the clock we must know the consciousness of the creature that uses the clock.

5

When we have gone this far we begin to realize that space and time are inextricably intermingled. They express themselves in terms of one another. Space is the time occupied, by whatever means, of getting from here to there. It seems much more helpful, when a man asks you how far it is to town, to find out what means of locomotion he possesses for getting there and then telling him how long it is going to take him. That is what he really wants to know: unless he intends to buy all the intervening land! An Indian will always tell you your journey in hours." The canal-Dutchman used to estimate their distance in "pipes," that is, the time it would take to smoke so many pipes of tobacco. It is quite a sensible procedure.

Similarly, though not quite so obviously, time may be expressed in terms of space. It is the radius of space occupied by any given consciousness.

This is not clear at first. But consider how in the course of our development we are continually reaching out to occupy more space. Our radius even of physical activity used to be very short. When we had to go afoot, without made paths, it was often ten or twenty miles only. That was as far from home as any but the most adventurous of us ever went. And the amount of space even the most adventurous could occupy was strictly limited by the length of his days. The hollowing of ships and the taming of horses helped a little. But even then, his habitual radius was only a trifle extended; and even were he to be an exceptional Marco Polo in his attainment of some far Cathay, the proportion of the earth's surface still closed to him must remain considerable. Since then we have gradually extended our circle. It is now possible for an enterprising man to occupy nearly the whole earth. The average is greatly widened. We are no longer as strictly local as we have been. Motors, airplanes, fast ships have helped us.

And we might go further and define the measure of our occupation as the speed by which we can cross its circle; and that is where the expression in the terms of time comes in. A man may have a general knowledge of the country covered by the widest journeying he may be able to accomplish; but he has not the intimate knowledge of occupancy until he can go quickly and frequently to all parts of his domain.

And we cannot confine these considerations to the merely physical. Man its likewise continually occupying more space by his thought. The primitive thinks only as far as he can see with his own two eyes: sometimes not even so far as that. Our astronomers think in terms of light years. There once more we return to the intermingled idea of space and time together.

6

This bring us inevitably to the conclusion that in any given instance time and space bear toward each other a fixed ratio. Each degree of consciousness has a rate of miles per hour, so to speak. Even among human beings this rate may vary somewhat. To another sort of consciousness the ratio, as we have seen, may be entirely different. To each sort of consciousness, however, it must be an exact and mathematical thing. In our own case it is, of course, the ratio between the circumference of our earth and the speed of its rotation. The latter allows us normally a fixed and definite period of time in which to do what we can with the former. We all understand that, and have grown into it, and condition ourselves accordingly. Because we understand it, we can intelligently comprehend the point of view as to duration and distance of all our fellow beings.

But when we attempt to observe or estimate after the manner of other sorts of consciousness than our own, we are at a loss. We do not know how long that two-second voyage of our microscopic creature seemed to him, either in time or space; and we have no means of finding out. We may estimate it by observing the duration of the vital processes and assuming a psychology to fit.

But we do not know. Why? *Because we do not know the ratio for this particular degree of consciousness.*

For there must be for him a ratio that is as mathematically exact as our own. It is the ratio peculiar to the circumstances of space which he has succeeded in occupying. Just as we, as human beings, have our own ratio; so our microscopical voyager must have his. And when we apply the ratio of one degree of consciousness to another, we merely confuse things; we unbalance things; we cannot possibly get other than a distorted intellectual image.

In order to understand any other degree of consciousness we would have to be able either to enter into and assume as our own its time and space ratio; or we would have to be able to manipulate it, as one manipulates a mathematical formula, so as to translate its concepts into something we can understand. Supposing the hypothetical inhabitants of Neptune to possess some ratio commensurate to their 165-year-long year, it is evident that even to communicate with them we must adapt or translate. If each of their seconds amounted to 165 of our seconds, and all their activities were gauged accordingly, our normal speech would be to them a meaningless blur. That is a simple physical example of what must be in reality much more complicated. The fling of thought itself is conditioned. The ability to know or handle other ratios is as yet beyond our power; but it must be a matter of exact mathematics, and it may be that in our own future we shall acquire command of it. Or it may well be that higher consciousnesses, if such exist, may already have command of it to a greater or lesser extent.

7

Like many powers-to-be this is curiously adumbrated in abnormal conditions. When the mathematical co-efficient is disturbed in the human brain by fever, or by certain drugs, it enters into or is partly influenced by other ratios than its own. These ratios may be either outside or inside its proper circle of occupation. A minute stretches to an hour; a night is years long. Events in vision seem to occur appropriately spaced with all the due leisure of actual happenings; and yet, while their apparent duration is days long, their actual perception may be within an hour. Some of the reactions to hashish illustrate this most strikingly. Cases have been reported where time has been speeded up—its ratio to space has been seriously altered—so that a man has seemed to himself to have been instantaneously transported from one side of a city to the other. Yet there was no lapse in perfect continuity. In another case the hashish eater has, as far as he was concerned, consumed several hours in a journey from his library door to his hearth. He had actually taken only as many seconds, yet all those inflated hours had been normally and completely and satisfactorily filled with incident. His circle of occupation had for the time being been contracted.

As I conceive it, the first thing our advanced student of the future would have to seek, when attempting—as he may—to enter for one purpose or another other degrees of consciousness than his own, would be the constant in the time and space ratio he seeks to use. There must always be such a constant: otherwise there must be infinite confusion. If mere subjectivity is to be the measure we have again to remember that no two beings see time alike. It flies or it drags. There must be a stable thing outside the individual to which to refer: a yardstick and a clock. We have adopted as our constant—or it has adopted us—the revolution of the earth, which has regularity, whatever else we may think about it. Similarly each degree of consciousness that has become self-consciousness in any degree, each circumference of occupied space, each ratio of time and space within that circumference must also have its constant. A knowledge of what this constant is must be prerequisite to understanding manipulation of the elements of time and space in any circumference whatever. We must know our twenty-four-hour day and its minutes and seconds, and we must know our capabilities of distance per second before we can estimate our journey. And any entity from some distant star, any degree of consciousness other than our own must know it also before it can come into understanding contact with us. We ourselves are acquainted at present with no other ratio than our own; and we are not as yet very skillful or at all final in our handling of that. We get better at it as we develop. We are constantly "annihilating" more space—and therefore time—as we progress.

Since we know neither the ratio nor the constant of other fields of consciousness than our own, we are quite unable to enter their fields of subjectivity. In simple words, we do not understand their point of view. To do that we would first of all have to possess the knowledge; and then we would have to manipulate our own ratio in such a manner as to make it correspond to theirs. That is one reason we cannot deliberately communicate with other degrees of consciousness as they communicate with each other.

Indeed, I conceive that if—as many believe—higher entities than ourselves do actually at times manage to communicate with some of us, this is one of the many difficulties that would make their communications fragmentary and unsatisfactory. It is conceivable—even probable—that their constant and ratio differ from our own. In that case we must assume, as a prerequisite for any communication whatever, that these entities, being of a higher development, have been able in some as yet imperfect way to translate their ratio into an approximation of ours. The thing must be mathematical. A complete knowledge of formula and method would of course permit a perfect manipulation, and consequently a perfect adaptation to our conditioning circumstances; and hence a perfect communicability. But suppose that even to these more advanced entities the knowledge is not quite completer Suppose the algebra of these equations is as yet imperfectly mastered?

Wherever that interesting train of thought might lead us, the result must be inevitably highly speculative. But from it we do get another slant at development; another definition to use when we come to the construction of our personal formula. Development, from this fresh angle, consists of an alternate reaching out to include more in the field of life, and then the bringing by one means or another of the scattered elements in that field into closer juxtaposition. We reached out to include more space when we adopted the automobile. By its means we then proceeded actually to bring the things within that space closer together. Measuring distance by time we made a twenty-mile square as compact a unit as was formerly a mile square. We might call this process a "Squeezing out" of space. It has been an invariable concomitant of development.

We can, starting from the microscopic organisms, trace a gradual expansion of field from the explorable vastness of a drop of water on the slide to the equally explorable spaces that separate the stars.

CHAPTER 21

THE OBJECT OF PRESSURE

~

1

NOW gradually, out of all the confusion of a few things known and many more guessed, we have arrived at a broad and general attitude toward ourselves. We see that we—in company with all the rest of creation—have at once an urge and an obligation toward development. That development is of ourselves and of the things with which we come into contact. The one is reciprocally dependent on the other. If we succeed in attaining a harmonious personal development, then by that very fact we help the rest of consciousness: if on the other hand we work along proper lines for the help of others, then that fact reacts in our favor personally. In whatever manner we have examined the field and method of this development—whether in space and time, in relation to the greater Consciousness, in relation to the quality of consciousness, or what not—we have found it to be invariably toward expansion, toward a wider inclusion. There is a resistless urge, a passion toward this. Sometimes that urge has translated itself as ambition, sometimes as mere discontent, sometimes as revolt. The discomfort that must accompany a function unfulfilled, an experiment incomplete, a balance not restored, we have variously named with synonyms for evil.

In this light we cannot but see that cruelty and injustice resolve themselves into stupidities; and the thing can still be stupid because it still is in the process of becoming. Furthermore, these pressures of discomforts of all sorts,—the necessity for toil, the necessity for combat, the necessity for resistance,—are lightened only when and to the degree that the equation is solved. Left to itself the human soul is naturally inert. It sits itself down under its banana tree and goes rapidly into a fatty degeneration. Only by pressures that induce rebound can it be roused to action. These pressures are inherent in the very incompleteness of the task; and the incompleteness comes to perception translated as evil and injustice, suffering and woe. Only thus are we made cognizant that something yet remains to be done.

And as any particular phase of the job nears completion, that particular pressure is lifted. We have improved our lot. Little by little, almost imperceptibly the coarser physical drudgeries are lifting. To be sure, in spite of great discoveries in the material world there is still much drudgery to be done; but some of the older crass pressures are no longer universally necessary and have been to an extent discarded. Famine, for instance. The Neanderthal man had, in all probability, to be constantly prodded by the fear of it. When he had a fresh kill he ceased from all effort; and if he could have been assured of an unfailing supply of meat, together with a warm safe place to eat it in, he would have been quite content never to do anything anymore. But the fact that he could quite literally starve and freeze kept him busy. In the modern world stark famine as a pressure has been much attenuated. Except as a catastrophe it no longer exists. It has been diluted down to the necessity to make a living; and in the majority of cases that in turn has been diluted to the desire to make the particular kind of living the individual wants.

This is a crude example; but it is a good one.

Not many of our fundamental pressures have been wholly lifted. We are not very far along yet in development. But a great many of them have been thinned, refined. There is considerable difference between the pain in the pit of the stomach the caveman felt when he failed to make his kill, and the pain in the conscience an upright man experiences when he fails his friend. There is a vast difference between the sort of toil that destroyed thousands of lives under the lash in the building of the pyramids, and the sort of toil that erects the modern skyscraper. None of these pressures, to repeat, has been wholly lifted. The socialist will tell you that some of the men who build the skyscraper are as much slaves to an industrial system as were the Egyptian slaves under the Pharaohs' taskmasters. Possibly so. Nevertheless, the slavery is not in so crude a form.

If the pressure still exists, it is because it is, broadly speaking, still necessary. That it is at times what we call an evil pressure is because it is an uncomfortable pressure. That it is uncomfortable is because that to which it appertains is still in the process of becoming, is still an object of experiment, of adjustment, of striving. The equation is not yet satisfied.

2

The object of pressure, then, is apparently to arouse. The emphasis of pressure, the degree of its discomforts, its miseries, its evils, its seemingly useless despair and tragedies and senseless cruelties against which we all cry out is an indication of the importance in the scheme of things of keeping alive at any sacrifice, at any cost, the flame of desire. No price is too great to pay for that. Nothing is of importance as compared to it. In the attainment of any primal necessity Nature always over-emphasizes, under-scores. She pours in reserves, and yet more reserves, to assure overwhelmingly the victory. That one animalcule carry on she creates millions; that one herring may reach the spawning shore she brings thousands into existence; that the race may go on she overloads the sexual instinct. She cannot afford to take chances; and rightly, for failure would be complete. The important thing is that Consciousness should progress in its finite aspect, becoming increasingly aware, pushing steadily and slowly but very surely toward its unknown unguessed goal. The job of being increasingly and expandingly Me must go on.

And in order that it go on the flame of desire must burn bright. That is vital because desire is vitality itself. The measure of its intensity is life: the measure of its absence is the degree of true death. All other considerations, in the very nature of things, pale into significance as compared to this. All other things depend on this.

Without that urge forward, that upspringing ever-renewed effort against inertia the scheme drops.

3

But though we can look forward to a gradual thinning of certain of the cruder pressures and resistances, and eventually to the entire removal of some of them, we cannot anticipate that all pressures will ever be lifted, so that we shall be eternally "at rest." Nor should we wish this to be the case. The airplane rises only by resistance, and would fall *in vacuo*. But it is one thing to fight blindly, and another thing to fight understandingly. The overcoming of resistances becomes a pleasurable function when one has obtained the command that comes from working in harmony. A skilled woodcarver enjoys his daily combat against the stubbornness of his material, whereas the small boy gets scant satisfaction from the woodpile ax.

It is not necessary to evoke a personal supervising intelligence in each and every instance to discover that as we show ourselves capable of remaining aroused, eager, vital, in the same proportion we are less spurred. The action is mechanical, reciprocating. Inertia brings swiftly applied pressure; pressure in turn arouses. An aroused spirit overcomes the inertia. And whenever the intricate web of life has brought it about that any pressure has been prematurely lifted, then we have observed a swift degeneration, a catastrophic lapse back, sometimes to the danger point. Occasionally this premature relief has been brought about in a small way, not by the effort of those immediately involved, but by the well-meant effort of others. The result has been the same. This is the profoundly basic reason why any wide scheme of ordinary "philanthropy" does not work; why the beneficent despotism does not work; why the indulgent parent does not work; why one cannot legislate virtue. Virtue is not an end in itself; it is a measure of growth. All one man can do for his fellow man is to help him toward keeping awake. Though here and there individual cases may be found—perhaps even in considerable numbers—where certain of the cruder pressures are still blindly applied beyond their time, the fact remains, by and large, that mankind *in general* is just about where it belongs in the scheme of things, and is rationed but little short of the point where it would be too apt to sit down content.

4

To many this will seem a harsh philosophy. It is not meant to be so; nor do I conceive that it really is so. That there is an inherent immediate injustice in many, perhaps even most, individual cases has little to do with it. The Scheme, as far as we have progressed in it, seems very young, very new. We represent rather crude beginnings. We know very little, and we have accomplished less, as compared to the possibilities of knowledge and of accomplishment. In our position we are relatively only as far along as the sand wasp's remote ancestors: we are still experimentally stabbing away, and perishing by the thousands. The injustice, and evil, and graft, and hatred, and cruelty, and wars, and other blind follies and extravagances are our failures. But we keep on stabbing! That is the important point. Our desire is still aflame and eager. And we are kept aflame and eager because of the necessities that drive us. Necessities will always drive us, world without end, amen. But we can conceive that in some remotely future estate they may be the joyous necessities of harmonious fulfilment rather than the harder necessities of mere maintenance. They will become so when by our struggle upward we make them so.

5

Some people see little hope in the situation. They look too closely about them. Their sympathies are enlisted, their imaginations filled by the troubles of men. War, pestilence, strife, inhumanity, oppression, greed, meanness, graft, corruption—all the destructive or deterrent forces—appear to them to be in the ascendant. Their minds are filled by and their tongues will quote the specific instance. They arrest the film for a detailed view; and the detailed view is not reassuring. But an arrested film is a picture of an absolute thing, a condition of affairs that is fixed: while this is a thing that is becoming. It moves; and it changes; and it has direction.

The movement is slow; despairingly slow if viewed from a single lifetime, or even the collective recollection of a people. But what can that matter, except to an individual viewpoint as expressed in a circumscribed manifestation? Whether a result is reached in ten years or ten thousand is important only to a certain time and space ratio. He who denies progress, even in the simpler humanities, is no student of history. Things are bad enough now; they were infinitely worse only the other day. We have here and there a criminal type of factory child labor, and it seems impossible to get adequate legislation against it. But it is not a widespread condition, public sentiment is actively opposed, and a vigorous fight is being made against it. Only a trifle over a century ago a little child was ordered deported to a criminal colony for carelessly tangling and breaking the bobbins of thread with which he was working. This was neither an isolated case of the sort, nor was it considered unusual or severe or unjustified. Not long before that Sir Philip Sidney was acclaimed as a most magnanimous warrior and so heralded throughout all Europe, so that his fame for gentleness of spirit has come down to us—largely on the basis of one deed. He gave to a wounded soldier the cup of water he was about to drink himself! It was a gracious and humane thing to do: probably Sir Philip was very dry after an arduous battle. The point of the matter is that at that time such an action was so unusual as to attract all that attention. A century or so ago, as a matter of course and openly, they imprisoned men most vilely for small debts, they hanged them for theft of the value of a few shillings. The medievalist was strictly and locally and everlastingly for himself alone. The thought of altruistic service had not dawned on him. Association for such service was practically unknown. And so on back. One with even a slender knowledge of detailed history of the sort that deals with something besides dates and kings and wars can hardly fall into the mistake of believing that things have not a motion and a change and a direction.

Some escape this conclusion by pointing to the fact that prototypes of all past evils exist actively today. That is true. Why not? In any organism—including the quality of consciousness we represent—all past history is both summed up and represented. There are cave men today, and medievalists, and predatory barons and all the rest of the crew. So are there protozoa and zoophytes and worms and mollusks and reptiles now flourishing just about as they used to flourish in all the stages of physical evolution back to the beginning. Probably there always will be. But we must remember that at one time the reptile, for example, was the highest and preponderating type of life. The fact that he still exists and carries on his affairs according to his reptilian ideas is no argument for the persistence of a reptilian world. Higher types of consciousness have evolved, and a different set of ideas, a different preponderating body of opinion has come into being.

The difference may be, acknowledgedly is, too slight. "The change may be, evidently is, almost dishearteningly slow. But there is change, there is movement, there is direction.

6

But, insists your pessimist, is there after all actual improvement? Externals may change, but human nature at bottom remains ever the same. When you dig down below the surface you will find the same medievalist, the same cave man at heart. Under stress of war, or famine, or danger of life, men quickly revert to primitive action and motive; civilization is only a thin veneer.

Of course! Why not? Human nature remains the same because human nature is nothing more nor less than the sum of all the attributes of the human quality. That sum must remain constant, or it would not make up the human quality. That is basic. Every one of the characteristics of the medieval man, of the cave man, must necessarily exist in us today. We may have brought to maturity many other, and higher characteristics, and we may have rendered important some that were formerly unimportant, but as far as the sum is concerned we have added nothing and subtracted nothing. Everything that makes us human exists and has existed—either matured, or in process, or in potentiality—in every one of us, since we became human; and will persist as long as we remain human. The proportions change, and the fields of action change. Attributes that have been merely potentialities in the cave man we have brought to the surface, and developed and learned to control. Attributes that were leading motives in the cave man we have—not changed or destroyed—but sublimated.

In that last word we find our answer to the pessimist. Freud and his school showed us the way, in their examination of one motive and attribute from among the many. We are by now thoroughly familiar with the process of sublimation by which the merely sexual instinct is raised in level, step by step, until it manifests itself in a high altruism. The number of esthetic perceptions alone that seem to be able to trace a direct pedigree to this one instinct is astonishing. The attribute of consciousness throughout remains the same: it merely changes its aspect and the conditions under which it works.

This has taken place in the history of the race: it often takes place in the individual, and by direct intention. It has now become a commonplace of treatment for those in whom the sexual instinct is too predominant. The urge is deliberately sublimated.

But though we all know about sublimation in this particular aspect, we are not so familiar with the thought that it not only applies to all other human attributes; but that it is a habitual process of evolution. Pure downright personal selfishness that grabs what it can, fights ruthlessly, and is quite devoid of a thought for anybody else on earth, soon extends to include the mate, then the children. It is still selfish, but in a double aspect. The primitive wishes to preserve the family for his own pleasure and comfort primarily; but he is selfish for them also a little on their own account. His ego has expanded to an inclusion. By progressive steps this grows to comprehend the camp, the village, the tribe, the nation. It goes beyond that. By a further process of sublimation it eventually includes sacrifice of one's intimate personal comfort or advantage for the sake of another. "I am not to be praised," disclaims such a man, "I am in reality acting selfishly because if I did not do this I would feel uncomfortable about it.' Pure selfishness has become, from one point of view, selflessness.) No conceivable human action can be imagined that may not, in this manner, be analyzed as enlightened self-interest.

Indeed, this sort of analysis is a favorite diversion of your pessimist. One whole school attempts to take the glory out of all esthetic and affectional impulse by reducing it to the sexual. It is a very simple matter similarly to label any constructive action as enlightened self-interest, thereby disparaging it by a name. The trick is both easy and plausible. But it ignores the most important idea of sublimation.

Similarly with the other attributes of human nature which have existed in the past. They have not changed in essential character, but they are all, every one of them, ever tending to work in thinner and thinner material; they are ever moving into a sublimation. Most of them are lamentably short; many of them have moved very little from their original estate. We should not expect anything different for the simple reason that as yet we are not very far along, wonderful as we sometimes think ourselves. But they have moved; they are moving.

7

And the conditions in which they manifest themselves are man's own work. He it is who has thinned the material. "To be sure," objects the pessimist, "the predatory industrial baron no longer as a matter of course everywhere exploits small children. But that does not indicate any great moral reform on his part. He merely hasn't the chance. If he had the chance, he'd do it quick as a wink." Precisely! And he has not the chance because public opinion, as a whole, has more or less effectively closed the chance; and public opinion in such basic matters is a measure of mankind's growth throughout effort. It has forced a sublimation of greed in this particular affair. The greed may be as yet pretty ugly, but it is not as ugly. The sublimation is very slight, but it is real. The predatory industrial baron may not have reformed his ideas; but he is forced by the advance of the body of consciousness to which he belongs to advance with it. And in time that fact even reacts on him. Predatory industrial barons are still predatory, but as a class they would not now dream of duplicating all the conditions of a hundred years ago, even had they the chance.

Again we must repeat, we cannot expect to eliminate the cave man any more than we should expect to find the elimination of all earlier steps in evolution. If there is, under our major hypothesis, to be a progressive elimination of forms of consciousness that have completed their job of being completely Me, that elimination must begin far down and work up. The different qualities of consciousness depend one on the other in lineage, pass one into the other in ascending continuity. There are a great many qualities of consciousness below that of the cave man. The supply of cave men, from below in the ascent, would seem to be sufficient. But we can expect slowly to raise the general average. At one time the cave man was the highest type. Then, although there were higher types, he still preponderated and established the conditions of life. Next those higher types tended toward predominance and established the conditions not only for the cave man, but for newer and still higher types as yet in the minority. Our hope is to continue this process: to produce, first of all, ever higher consciousness; then to increase the number of the individuals possessing that consciousness to the point where they will make the conditions. And so on up. That is what I mean in essence by public opinion. Its average establishes the conditions for the action of the human attributes, whatever they may be. Its average is the measure of our progress.

So when we say that A would grab, steal, lie, bite, scratch and gouge in the good old way, only he has not now the chance, we are merely trying to place A in evolution. We are labelling him individually. If we would label the human race we must define the chance.

Many of even the simplest conditions under which a certain small degree of sublimation is working have not been stabilized. They are easily overset; and then we revert temporarily to old conditions. When that happens we find in dominance the people, or the kind of motives, or the ideas that were normally dominating the old conditions. But the lapses, serious as they may be, are in the long run temporary. And it is to be noted that the reversion is, broadly speaking, in conditions and not in degrees of consciousness. Merely, for the time being, the most advanced class resumes the place that it formerly had occupied,—as too far ahead to represent the average of public opinion.

So pessimism is, after all, merely the taking of too narrow a view. When things are dark, just extend the horizon. If one continues far enough, he is bound to come upon clear skies at last.

CHAPTER 22

EPILOGUE

~

1

WE seem now, however inadequately, to have traversed the field we had laid out for ourselves. That is, we have made some sort of an attempt at an accounting for the universe which is intellectually satisfying; we have placed ourselves in that universe; we have determined a movement, indicated a direction. Above all, we have tried to show that the outlook is hopeful. These are all assistants toward orientation. Once a man is oriented, he must go ahead by his own compass.

Therefore, this little volume comes logically to its end. Further speculation would enter different fields. We should next have to examine man's relations with himself, and man's relations with his fellow men. The first would include spiritual hygiene, in all that it implies of development, equipment and method. The second would comprise ethics and the mechanism of communication in the broadest sense; struggle, and cooperation. If the present volume happens to arouse enough interest in these purely personal beliefs of mine, I may go on to discuss these questions in subsequent works. In the meantime, my strongest advice is, that by whatever means most appeals, each human being establish his direction. He must do this before he can begin to move, except aimlessly and in dependence on lucky chance.

APPENDIX

~

1

D R. ALLEN'S report was read before the British Association for the Advancement of Science at their Hull Meeting in 1922. This report is difficult to obtain, so for the benefit of the curious reader I here epitomize the argument as briefly as possible.

It has been found that light in very short wave lengths acting on sea water and carbon dioxide produces formaldehyde with liberation of free oxygen. Light of slightly longer wavelength causes the molecules of formaldehyde to unite to form simple sugars. By light of a still different wavelength nitrates are converted to the more chemically active nitrites. Nitrites have been united with active formaldehyde by subjecting the mixture to light from a quartz mercury lamp. The result is a nitrogenous organic substance.

That, so to speak, is the first cycle. We have the spectacle of *organic* substance formed directly from sea water by the action of light waves of different lengths. These wave lengths are not available in sunlight as we know it in the present day.

But it is quite possible that they were present in some past phase of earth evolution, when organic substance may be conceived to have come into existence. Furthermore, it has been found that certain colors have the property of making even present day sunlight active in this respect. These colors have been named photocatalysts, and may have been present in the atmosphere or the sea water at the beginning of organic substance. This is the first step: the formation of organic substance without the intervention of living organisms.

The organic substance (for reasons derived from pure physics) would take the colloid state.

Now the electric charges on this surface of colloid particles would produce absorption, and fresh ions would be attracted from all about.

Thus we have now a mass of colloid, differing in surface tension from the sea water, and increasing in size by two processes: (1) chemical, from the linkage of carbon atoms; and (2) physical, from the absorption of ions.[1]

Obviously, the surface tension of this colloid substance must be slightly different from that of the surrounding sea water.

The difference in surface tension would tend to make the surface of the colloid as small as possible, which tendency, if unchecked, would result in a sphere. But the tendency toward growth would, on the other hand, demand as large a surface as possible in order to facilitate exchange with the surrounding medium. Thus we have a conflict. The result is a tendency for the mass to break up into minute particles at the slightest agitation, and to change form wherever by growth local alterations in surface tension are brought about.

The building up process,—which, it must be remembered, is dependent on light waves—would be subject to the alterations of night and day. At night, naturally, light, the supply of energy, would be removed. In order to delay to an extent the resultant onset of what is called molecular finality some sort of reaction must continue, even though at a lower rate, until the following day brings back the light waves again. The thing has to be kept going. Since, obviously, this cannot be through energy from without, it must be through energy from within. The only way energy can be released from within is by some sort of breaking down process, just as heat is released from coal by its breaking down under oxygenation. The colloidal plasma for the first time exhibits an adaptation. It has previously been merely chemical proteid matter. Now it "becomes an autotropic, increasingly self-regulated, and so far individualized entity." Autotropic means simply "capable of self-nourishment."

Next this plasma differentiates naturally, from the mere fact of its position as respects the source of light into different layers. The first is in molecular contact with the water, from which it receives substances in the form of ions, and to which it gives off ions. The next is a self-nourishing layer to which light penetrates under whose influence new

[1] Colloid—merely the antithesis of crystalloid.

organic substance is formed in the manner we have sketched. And third, a center to which light does not penetrate, and which also is cut off from the surrounding medium. The latter, having no other means of support, is forced to depend on the outside layers for its nutrition. And in consequence it is itself concerned only with the breaking down process of producing energy.

Already, as we see, this thing is acquiring specialized functions. It is also acquiring shape. The part nearest the light grows faster than the part in the shadow. Therefore, the original sphere becomes elongated. The thing has definite ends. And with the concentration at the nucleus the specific gravity of the plasma exceeds that of the water. It tends to sink. But as that would remove it from the light, on which it depends, another adaptation is necessary. We see the part of the external layer which les nearest the light becoming contractile and moving rhythmically. This makes a tractor that tends to draw the plasma toward the source of light, and so prevent sinking.

But while this adaptation was in process the loss must have been enormous. Probably only in comparatively shallow waters could the organism survive. There must have been a constant shower of moribund plasma sinking toward the ocean bed. If by chance one of these moribund plasma happened to come against one more vigorous it would coalesce with the latter, as two drops merge. That would be a kind of feeding. Or if two moribund plasma, both sinking, should come in contact, they too would coalesce; and the combined energy of the two might result in revivication. That would be conjugation— analogous to a sort of sexual fusion.

Again, in shallow water it would often happen that an organism would run aground and stick to the bottom. The tractor would go on working; only now, instead of drawing the organism upward, it would tend to suck the sea water downward. If weaker organisms happened into the current thus formed they would drift down and the two would coalesce. Thus ingestion and animal nutrition would in these cases gradually take preponderance over mere plant growth. We have a true animal.

Dr. Allen goes farther into other considerations—such as the imperative necessity of shallow water for any development whatever— but this is the gist of his report as respects the development of life from ordinary sea water and light.

CREDO

2

The pedinella is a floating flagellate which nourishes itself in typical plant fashion, i.e. by chemical change of mineral substance under the influence of light through chromatophores—color cells. It possesses a sort of trailing fringed stalk which has to do with its tractor arrangements. But occasionally this stalk causes it to run aground. The pedinella then begins to feed as an animal, by ingestion. After this has continued for some time, the chromatophores practically disappear.

THE END